Don't Tell Cute Stories –
Change Lives!

"*Don't Tell Cute Stories* is much more than a Happy Meal! It's the extra large Big Mac meal of books designed to raise champion children in the 21st century. It covers the lot – why to and how to, when to and where to. It's fully comprehensive.

"Buy the book and take children's ministry out of the hands of babysitters and into the hands of fully-equipped commandos, determined to explode it onto the centre stage of every church programme."

Dave Gilpin
Senior Minister, Hope City Church, Sheffield

"Another great resource for children's workers from Mark Griffiths. If he keeps going like this I'm going to need more shelf space!"

Doug Horley (Duggie Dug Dug)

"The excellent material presented in this book is clearly based on years of experience in children's ministry, and offers a wealth of wisdom and insight into evangelising and discipling boys and girls. It succeeds in demonstrating relevant and contemporary teaching methods, as well as being practical and promoting good and safe practice in children's ministry. This book will inspire children's workers to think bigger, believe for greater things and see little lives changed."

Steve Williams
National Director of Children's Ministries
Assemblies of God in Great Britain and Ireland

"Mark's book gives us both a strategic framework for children's work, as well as tried-and-tested practical applications and outworking. All this, plus some great stories and inspiring testimonies, ensures this is definitely one for the desk and not the shelf."

Helen Shannon
Director of New Wine Children's Ministry

"Very good ... I had to stop and pray ... Mark not only challenges us, but encourages us to be both realistic and visionary. This is the book for Now. Mark shows us how to relate to today's generation in an effective and culturally relevant way ... his pithy humour cuts through and kicks the point well into the back of the net."

Rev. Jim Bailey
Kingdom Creative (EAC)

Don't Tell Cute Stories –
Change Lives!

Mark Griffiths

MONARCH
BOOKS
Mill Hill, London & Grand Rapids, Michigan

First published in 2003 in the UK by Monarch Books, Concorde House,
Grenville Place, Mill Hill, London NW7 3SA.

Distributed by:
UK: STL, PO Box 300, Kingstown Broadway, Carlisle, Cumbria CA3 0QS;
USA: Kregel Publications, PO Box 2607, Grand Rapids, Michigan 49501.

ISBN 1 85424 624 0 (UK)
ISBN 0 8254 6231 2 (USA)

British Library Cataloguing Data
A catalogue record for this book is available
from the British Library.

Designed and produced for the publishers by
Gazelle Creative Productions Ltd,
Concorde House, Grenville Place, Mill Hill, London NW7 3SA.

DEDICATION

This book is dedicated to Rev. George R. Ridley – who sharpened me as iron sharpens iron – the senior minister at Christian Centre, Milton Keynes, where I enjoyed eleven years and learnt many valuable lessons.

And to Rev. Dr Mike Archer and the team at St Mary's, Bletchley, who have welcomed my family and me so warmly, and where we have learnt so much so quickly. We hope that we can prove to be a blessing to you also.

ACKNOWLEDGEMENTS

A big thank you to my wife, Rhian, and my friends Laura Conway, Phil Craythorne, Pamela Currie, Louise Davies and David Ritchie – each of them amazing children's workers in their own right – who took the time to read through the original manuscript, commented honestly and allowed me to use the many items that were undoubtedly their ideas in the first place.

And to the thousands of children and children's workers in whose lives I have had the privilege of being involved.

Children of The Cross

God is raising up an army
Made of those who are still young
God is lifting up their voices
Through the weak he'll shame the strong
It's been prophesied, they will prophesy
God's salvation they will show
For the promise is to the children
To our daughters and our sons

Children of the cross, a shining example
Children of the cross are singing his praise
Children of the cross are silencing the enemy
Children of the cross are saying the Lord saves

© 1997 Jim Bailey

FOREWORD

You are holding in your hands a remarkable book. When I first read the manuscript I knew immediately that I simply could not wait to get this into the hands of all the children's workers at St Luke's. Previously books on the subject of evangelism amongst children have been worthy, but not inspiring. Usually their impact on me has been to make me feel guilty, but not to release me into greater effectiveness.

This book is different. In it Mark manages to convey his own infectious enthusiasm for evangelism amongst children. He makes a compelling case for the strategic value of such work. He provides great ideas and lots of helpful comments. Reading this will certainly put a smile back on the face of a weary children's worker. However, it will do more than that. It will impart to ministers like me, vicars and pastors and leading elders, something of the passion for this vital work that Mark himself feels. Having imparted the passion, it then gives enough pointers as to what to do and how to achieve it that even the most ignorant local church should be able to embark on effective kids' club evangelism.

If you buy no other book about child evangelism, sell your shirt and buy this one. Seriously, I pray that it will be used by God to release hundreds of churches in this country into strategic and powerful evangelism among children. It certainly has all the potential to do so.

Eric Delve
Vicar and Team Leader, St Luke's, Maidstone, Kent

CONTENTS

The Beginners' Guide

The Extra Stuff

A WORD FROM THE AUTHOR

Churches all over the UK and across the western world are beginning to see the important role that they can play in instilling strong moral and spiritual values into the lives of children. Concepts of salvation, honesty, trust, love, kindness and self-control are being taught in fun and interesting ways in children's clubs and Sunday schools. One little twelve-year-old girl from Milton Keynes wrote:

> *Our children's club is great. When I was six I never knew who God was and if he ever even existed. Since I have been coming here I now know about God and everything that goes with it...*

Incidentally, the same girl has just become a junior leader in the same children's club.

The common thread seems to be learning and enjoyment running side by side – bouncy castles, computer games, pool and snooker alongside stories, Bible lessons and passionate preaching.

There are several elements that are involved in the equation that equals excellent children's clubs. They could ultimately boil down to just two:

- Gifting
- Hard Work

Over the last couple of years I have discovered a relationship between these two factors. It would appear that the harder I work, the more gifted I become!

This book is packed full of ideas that I am convinced (if applied correctly) will help your children's club grow. The "Alpha to Omega" section is a proven template for establishing high attendance, community impact and purposeful discipleship. However there are some things that can't be purchased in book form. The Bible makes it clear in Proverbs 21:5:

> *Good planning and hard work lead to prosperity, but hasty shortcuts lead to poverty.* (NLT)

There is no substitute for hard work. Take the principles outlined in this book, consider the pattern in the latter pages, prayerfully consider all that you would do, but ultimately without hard work you will not achieve.

Not every part of the book will be useful for you; other parts will be life-changing. And what is useful and what is not will vary from person to person. Prayerfully throw away the bones but hold tight to the meat.

You never know, there may be the means within this book to take you to a whole new level of children's ministry. I sincerely believe that for many that is exactly what this book will do.

This book is about children's clubs – about a heartfelt belief that Christian children's clubs in the heart of every community can have a dynamic effect on those communities and cause our churches to grow.

Mark Griffiths
May 2003

The Why

MIDNIGHT WALKS AND DAISY CHAINS
(How I got into Children's Work)

It was my final year in theological college and, like many other students, I had been wondering what the future would hold. It was a cold night and the rain hadn't stopped for several days. By now it was approaching midnight and, lying in my bed, I found the rain hammering against the window comforting. I was beginning to drift off to sleep when I felt I heard God speak. I had been a Christian for only six years, and had spent the last three at college, but I knew when God was saying something.

"Do you really care about the young people and children of this nation?"

"God, you know that I do," I instantly responded.

The conversation continued:

"If you really care then I want you to pray now."

I rolled out of the quilt and knelt beside my bed. I had begun to pray when God prompted once again.

"If you pray there you will be asleep."

I know that God knows all things, but I don't think he was particularly stretched in that revelation. I pulled on my clothes and suggested to God that we could probably do this tomorrow if he wasn't too busy. Still, I ventured out into the wet night and made my way to one of my favourite prayer spots, a footpath bridge that crossed over a river. It took me less than ten minutes to get there, but by the time I arrived I was very wet. There was certainly no chance of dropping off to sleep, but I also didn't much feel like praying – I was wet and cold. The rain was still hammering down and the river looked particularly rough. The only prayer I was praying was, "God, what am I doing standing here?". There was no response.

I stood for a little longer and was about to make my way back when I saw two other students walking towards me. Contrary to urban legend it is not commonplace for theological students to be walking around at midnight in the rain, let alone to find three of them out at the same time. They approached me and asked:

"Did you hear a scream?"

I shook my head. I hadn't heard anything except the wind and the river. We concluded that it must have been someone having a nightmare back at the college. They nodded and asked if I was OK, and when I nodded they made their way back to college. I stood a little longer and was about to make my way back when God spoke again, this time more clearly than I had ever heard him before, or since. He said:

"The sound that I hear is a constant scream, the scream as millions of children are aborted before they are born, the scream as they are hurt and abused, the scream as they feel helpless and that nobody cares, the scream as they feel lost and alone and carry those scars into their adult lives, the scream as relationship after relationship lets them down and the ultimate scream as they topple helplessly and alone towards hell."

By now I was wet to the skin, shivering with the cold, and if anything the rain was coming down faster and the wind blowing more ferociously. But I didn't care about the wind or the rain, I had felt something that God feels; I had shared for a micro-second an inkling of the pain that Father God feels and for a brief moment I understood how desperate God was to reach these children.

"God," I prayed, "I want to make a difference. Use me to reach these children, use me."

I prayed and kept on praying. The rain continued to fall, the wind continued to blow and I continued to pray, into the night I prayed...

Amy Carmichael was a missionary in the 19th century. One night she had a dream. In her dream she found herself on the edge of a cliff. Far below she could see the waves hammering onto the rocks. And as she stood there she saw people rushing towards the edge of the cliff. She ran back and forth trying to stop them falling off the cliff. She managed to rescue many but she couldn't get to them all.

Then she noticed that not far from the cliff's edge there were people sitting on picnic blankets, making daisy chains. In her dream Amy shouted to them to try to get some help, but they didn't move, they continued making daisy chains. Amy continued running back and forth and then she woke up.

She asked God what it meant and then she understood. The people were walking and toppling over the cliff towards hell and she was rescuing them. Those who sat and made daisy chains represented the church of her day, apathetic and ineffective, content with their own pastimes and having no interest in the lost world outside.

Amy committed her life to patrolling the edge of that cliff and rescuing as many as she could. She opened many orphanages in India and rescued literally hundreds of children from idolatry.

I do not believe that the church today is the same as the church in Amy's day. I genuinely believe that for the most part we have conquered apathy and complacency. Our biggest enemy today is not indifference; our biggest enemy today is activity! We are all too busy doing something.

It would appear that we are no longer making daisy chains, but we also didn't take the step of standing on the cliff top. Instead, we decided to set up rescue shelters at the bottom of the cliff. We wait until people fall onto the rocks and then we try to help them. We wait until their lives are in pieces and then we offer to put them back together. We are keen to repair men and women. In the 21st century the church has some of the best counselling services available. We can counsel drug addicts, we can counsel alcoholics, we can counsel those who are having relationship problems, we can counsel those who were bullied at school… Pick a problem and we have a counselling service for it! Lots and lots of activity, lots of people working furiously at the bottom of the cliff but very few at the top. One man put it like this:

"It is better to build up boys and girls than repair men and women."

My grandmother put it another way:

"Prevention is always better than cure."

Children's ministry stands at the top of the cliff with arms wide. *It is about building strong children, making them secure, introducing them to a God who loves them,* showing them a godly example and convincing them that they have a destiny that God set apart for them even before he began to put the universe together. The Bible leaves us in no doubt that the devil comes to kill, steal and destroy – to kill innocence, to steal destiny and to destroy lives. It is sheer stupidity to watch as the devil does these things and then some years later try to repair the damage. We must reach children before they hit the rocks. We must stand at the edge of the cliff. The tragedy is that 80% of the church's resources are still being poured into repairing men and women. We must work to change this, but as we work we must stand at the edge of the cliff.

Our churches glamorise and sensationalise the man or woman whose life was in ruins on the rocks and then was put back together. Those who were drug addicts, murderers, thieves and muggers pack our arenas as they tell how God changed their lives and I cheer with everyone else. I stand in awe at the grace of God, but I take great exception at those who then mutter:

"Wasn't that a great testimony?"

The answer is "no". That was not a great testimony. It was great to see God changing a life; it was great to see the Holy Spirit drawing a sinner back to Christ, but it was not a great testimony. Great testimonies are those where a person stands and tells of how they gave their life to Jesus at a very young age and they felt God speaking to them and they lived their life for him and they became a doctor, or engineer, or miner, or missionary and served God all their lives. The devil didn't get a chance to destroy anything – now that's a great testimony. It's not so dramatic; it may never pack arenas, but never let go of the fact that this is what we should be aiming for.

I am not advocating that we close our counselling centres: there will always be those that slip through and better that we reach them later on than that we don't reach them at all. But, at the same time, let's keep the ultimate aim in our minds – reaching boys and girls.

God, let me so inspire a generation of people that they will stretch their arms across the edge of the cliff. Even if that never happens, I will stand at the edge of the cliff and I will make a difference.

HE'LL BE A PROPER MINISTER ONE DAY
(Why I stayed involved in Children's Work)

"That was a very good sermon this morning. He'll be a proper minister one day."

I had just ministered to 20 people in a Sunday morning service. The minister of this particular church pointed out that the numbers were low as several people were away and others were unwell. He assured me that on a good Sunday he could have as many as 30. I had been invited to come and preach an inspirational sermon in the morning and talk on children's ministry in the evening. I had completed my first task and was at the minister's home for Sunday lunch.

"He'll be a proper minister one day."

These words weren't spoken to me – they never are. They were the words of encouragement the minister had for my wife while I was visiting the bathroom. It's a common view: I showed "potential", so surely I would graduate to bigger and better things soon. My dilemma was that I didn't want to graduate. And it was a real dilemma. I had prayed and asked God for guidance, but I just didn't hear God telling me to leave the wonderful arena of children's ministry. Many had pointed out that children's ministry wasn't even a biblical concept; they were respected individuals, so I believed them. So what was I doing? I searched the Bible to find out for myself if there was a biblical basis for children's ministry.

What resulted was not a sudden revelation that I should now become a "proper" minister, but a clearer and more holistic understanding of what children's ministry in the 21st century needed to be about.

One of the first mentions of children is found in Deuteronomy 6:5–7:

So love the LORD your God with all your heart, soul, and strength. Memorise his laws and tell them to your children over and over again. Talk about them all the time, whether you're at home or walking along the road or going to bed at night, or getting up in the morning.

The same point is emphasised in Deuteronomy 11:18–19:

Memorise these laws and think about them. Write down copies and tie them to your wrists and your foreheads to help you obey them. Teach them to your children. Talk about them all the time – whether you're at home or walking along the road or going to bed at night, or getting up in the morning.

The context is clear. Teaching and instruction in these verses are to take place in the home, with parents teaching and instructing their own children. The verses show when that teaching should occur – "talk about them all the time". Not only are the children to be taught in the home, not only are they to learn about it every day, but they are also to be made aware of it in their daily lives, when they walk along the road, when they go to bed at night.

In a practical sense it means that when I'm walking home with my daughter in the early evening I will encourage her to look up and I will say:

"Hey, Nia, look at those stars. God put them there. The Bible says that the skies show God's glory."

A natural occurrence being used to show the greatness of our God.

Exodus adds another dimension in its directions for the Passover in Exodus 12:21–28:

Each family is to pick out a sheep and kill it for Passover. Make a brush from a few small branches of a hyssop plant and dip the brush in the bowl that has the blood of the animal in it. Then brush some of the blood above the door and on the posts at each side of the door of your house. After this, everyone is to stay inside. During that night the LORD will go through the country of Egypt and kill the firstborn son in every Egyptian family. He will see where you have put the blood, and he will not come into your house. His angel that brings death will pass over and not kill your firstborn sons. After you have entered the country promised to you by the LORD, you and your children must continue to celebrate Passover each year. Your children will ask you, "What are we celebrating?" And you will answer, "The Passover animal is killed to honour the LORD. We do these things because on that night long ago the LORD passed over the homes of our people in Egypt. He killed the firstborn sons of the Egyptians, but he saved our children from death." After Moses finished speaking, the people of Israel knelt down and worshipped the LORD. Then they left and did what Moses and Aaron had told them to do.

God knows that children are incredibly inquisitive:

"When your children ask you, 'what are we celebrating?'". He designed them that way, with a thirst for truth, and when they asked, God wanted them to hear the account of the Passover, the account of an all-powerful God who had led his people out of a foreign land into a land flowing with milk and honey.

The pattern repeats in Joshua 4:2–8:

Tell one man from each of the twelve tribes to pick up a large rock from where the priests are standing. Then have the men set up those rocks as a monument at the place where you camp tonight. Joshua chose twelve men; he called them together, and told them: Go to the middle of the river bed where the sacred chest is, and pick up a large rock. Carry it on your shoulder to our camp. There are twelve of you, so there will be one rock for each tribe. Some day your children will ask, "Why are these rocks here?" Then you can tell them how the water stopped flowing when the chest was being carried across the river. These rocks will always remind our people of what happened here today.

The men followed the instructions that the LORD had given Joshua. They picked up twelve rocks, one for each tribe, and carried them to the camp, where they put them down.

God tells his people to take twelve rocks out of the water as they cross (there is an important lesson in this account that we will return to at the end of this chapter). The stones are to be set up as a memorial so that those inquisitive children can ask what the memorial refers to.

God wants these children to know that he is a God who does things. A God who holds back the river so that his people can cross over; a God who does miracles; a God who wants to be involved in the lives of his people.

And so the Old Testament picture is one of:

- **Children taught by their parents**
- **Children taught every day**
- **Children taught through examples from their everyday lives**
- **Children taught that this is not an abstract God, but a God who is involved with his people**
- **Children taught that this is a God of miracles**

But it would be wrong of us to assume that God is only interested in information and knowledge being communicated from parent to child. *It is much more explosive than that. This is about the communication of living faith, a hot, passionate belief in a God who can change lives, who can rescue his people, who operates in the supernatural.*

The difficulty facing the Old Testament Jewish parents was clear: if they didn't have this passionate relationship with God then they would not be able to communicate it to their children. So we can add to this list:

- **Children seeing a passionate and living faith in their parents**

Having described the Old Testament pattern, it might appear that the critics were correct that there is no biblical basis for children's ministry as we understand it. Don't resign yet; there is hope. It is important for us to understand the Old Testament pattern, the ideal, and although we may never live in the ideal we need to be aware of it and to work towards it. The ideal pattern, as scripture presents it, is parents imparting living faith into the lives of their children.

In a Christian home this should be what we are aiming for. It is my responsibility to impart living faith to my children. The Sunday school teacher complements what I do, but does not replace it.

If we now apply Old Testament patterns to our 21st century context, and add to it the disturbing fact that only 1 in every 13* UK children has any contact with church or church groups, then we begin to understand our new role.

For those children who have Christian parents with a living faith, the burden and responsibility of scripture is clear – their parents have been ordained by God to teach and instruct their children. But, for the millions of children who have no Christian parents from whom to draw this living faith, God has chosen you, not to be the Sunday school teacher or the children's club leader or the children's pastor, but to be a spiritual foster parent to those children who are desperate for this living faith, this love that glows like molten lava, which God is desperate to pour into these young lives. *You are it to this generation.* If you will not introduce them to the God who loves them as much as he loved his own Son, to the God who allowed the ultimate sacrifice to enable them to draw close to him, then they may be lost.

Spiritual foster parents need to understand the Old Testament pattern in a modern context:

- **Children taught by their Christian parents and spiritual foster parents**
- **Children taught every day (it's got to be more than the one-hour slot once a week)**
- **Children taught through examples from their everyday lives**
- **Children taught that this is not an abstract God, but a God who is involved with his people**
- **Children taught that this is a God of miracles**
- **Children seeing a passionate and living faith in their parents/spiritual foster parents**

• Statistics provided by Child Evangelism Fellowship

It is worth returning to the ideal. The ideal is Christian parents imparting living faith. So we work ourselves out of a job. We reach boys and girls who do not have Christian parents; we impart living faith to them and they develop their own relationship with God. In years to come they may marry and have children of their own. But now the emphasis is different: their children don't need spiritual foster parents, because they have parents with living faith. You just broke into a family line and changed the pattern. From then on that family line will work on parents imparting living faith to their children. Back to the ideal.

King Josiah is a miracle. His father is an evil man; his grandfather is an evil man. But Josiah proves to be one of the most righteous kings Israel will see. How is this possible? The interesting thing is this: when Josiah is talked about he is mentioned as having the same faith as "his father David".

Clearly David is not his father. But David is the man from whom Josiah draws his godly example. Herein lies the pattern. We are to become those from whom children can draw their example. Children who can say that they have the same faith as their father, Jack or Jim or Mary or Sue...

There was a very interesting piece of research done which underlines the need and shows us something more. When we reach a generation, we don't just change their lives but we also touch the future. Two family trees were traced. The first belonged to Jonathan Edwards, a preacher born in 1703. His descendants contain:

- 300 ministers
- 65 professors
- 13 university presidents
- 16 authors
- 1 United States president

As another example, Ada Take was born in 1740. She was a drunk and made her living through prostitution. Her descendants contain:

- 100 women pregnant out of wedlock
- 181 prostitutes
- 152 beggars
- 46 dropouts
- 76 involved in serious crime

We need to break into the family trees of the Ada Takes of this world and make a difference in order to change the destiny of a whole succession of generations.

Back to Joshua: in Joshua 3:10 – 4:7 we read:

And now, God is going to prove that he's powerful enough to force them out. Just watch the sacred chest that belongs to the LORD, the ruler of the whole earth. As soon as the priests carrying the chest step into the Jordan, the water will stop flowing and pile up as if someone had built a dam across the river.

The LORD has also said that each of the twelve tribes should choose one man to represent it. The Israelites packed up and left camp. The priests carrying the chest walked in front, until they came to the River Jordan. The water in the river had risen over its banks, as it often does in springtime. But as soon as the feet of the priests touched the water, the river stopped flowing, and the water started piling up at the town of Adam near Zarethan. No water flowed toward the Dead Sea, and the priests stood in the middle of the dry river bed near Jericho while everyone else crossed over.

After Israel had crossed the Jordan, the LORD said to Joshua: Tell one man from each of the twelve tribes to pick up a large rock from where the priests are standing. Then have the men set up those rocks as a monument at the place where you camp tonight.

Joshua chose twelve men; he called them together, and told them: Go to the middle of the river bed where the sacred chest is, and pick up a large rock. Carry it on your shoulder to our camp. There are twelve of you, so there will be one rock for each tribe. Some day your children will ask, "Why are these rocks here?" Then you can tell them how the water stopped flowing when the chest was being carried across the river. These rocks will always remind our people of what happened here today.

Joshua tells the priests to enter the water and stand. The Bible then tells us that the water started to pile up some 20km upstream at a place called Adam. The water didn't pile up several metres away from the priests; it was 20km away, so before the people could cross over 20km worth of rubbish had to flow past the priests first. And this would be a colourful array of rubbish, for all sorts of interesting refuse would have flowed into the river. But the priests did not move. They stood firm while the junk and garbage of society flowed over them, so that the nation could move over safely.

And so to you, fellow children's worker: **are you ready to allow the rubbish that this society throws at you, and some rubbish that the church throws at you, to flow past so that you can win a generation?** Are you prepared to stand firm so that many can be won?

And there will always be those who in condescending tones will pronounce that you will move to a proper ministry one day – that's part of the rubbish you have to stand through; there will be those who will never understand. But, ultimately, who cares how much rubbish we have to stand through? Don't be sidetracked by the rubbish; there are boys and girls being abused right now who have a chance of healing because of who you are and what you do. There are children who now have a chance of eternal life because of what you do. There are boys and girls who would have grown up to be drug dealers and dangerous criminals, who would have wasted their lives, but won't now, because of who you are and what you do. Because you have been called by God to be a spiritual foster parent, to stand firm as the rubbish rushes past you.

This book is about evangelism; it's about reaching out; it's about purposeful discipleship and it's about releasing a generation of children fully alive to God's Spirit.

The How

BUILD IT BIG

The previous chapters were very important. They reinforce my passionate belief that burden gives birth to vision. If we never truly see the need then we will never have a strong enough desire to meet the need. So, there are four stages in developing a thriving children's work that has the ability to produce children who love Jesus in ever increasing numbers.

1. **Burden** ... God opening our eyes to see the need
2. **Vision** ... A God-given strategy to meet the need
3. **Goals** ... God-given methods for working the vision out
4. **Perseverance** ... The sheer determination to see it through

Burden

The process must begin with burden. If your heart is not in this then you must pray and ask God to reveal something of *his* heart. You cannot jump stages; if you don't feel the need with an intensity that wrenches at your heart then you have not seen the situation as God sees it. *Tearless eyes never gave birth to God-given vision.* It is the basis of our motivation; it is the seedbed of vision; it is our reason for being. If Nehemiah had never been stirred by the state of the walls in Jerusalem he never would have had the vision to do anything about their restoration. Jesus looked at Jerusalem and uttered:

> *Jerusalem, Jerusalem! Your people have killed the prophets and have stoned the messengers who were sent to you. I have often wanted to gather your people, as a hen gathers her chicks under her wings.*
> (Matthew 23:37)

Vision

So, if we have a burden then we can begin to pray and ask God what part he wants us to play in meeting this need – to give us vision. A warning at this point from the prophet Jeremiah:

God said to Jeremiah in Jeremiah 2:13:

> *You, my people, have sinned in two ways – you have rejected me, the source of life-giving water, and you've tried to collect water in cracked and leaking pits dug in the ground.*

The prophet is rebuking the people for rejecting God and trying to dig their own wells to gain water. Instead of trusting God, they have tried to solve the problem themselves. An easy trap to fall into: we see the need and we race to meet this need. We feel a deep concern for drug addicts and we open a drug-counselling agency. There is clearly a balance to be struck here. If we see a starving child, we don't need an angel from heaven to visit us before we decide to feed him, but, at the same time, if we forget to involve God in our plans and schemes then it will not ultimately make the difference it could. Lots of projects have been conceived in God's name and yet God knows very little about them. There is strength and a certitude and a peace that come from knowing that the work you are involved in was given to you by God.

Vision is important. We need to know where we are going. These wonderful lines from *Alice in Wonderland* illustrate the point well:

> *"Would you tell me please which way I should go from here?" asked Alice.*
> *"That depends a good deal on where you want to get to," said the Cat.*

We know God wants us to have more than this; we know God wants to take us on from here; we know in our heart of hearts that we're not content with the level of our children's ministry, and we desperately want to take it somewhere else. But where?

The dialogue between the Cat and Alice continues with Alice explaining that she doesn't much care where she gets to as long as it is away from here. The Cat assures her that if she keeps walking she's sure to do that. And that is the general shape of children's ministry at the start of the 21st century. We all want something more, but we have no idea what. We don't like where we are but we don't know what we want instead. We know we want to move from here but we don't know where to. So we keep doing what we're doing, hoping it will get better soon. The problem with this philosophy is simple:

- *We don't know where we want to go*
- *We won't recognise it when (or if) we get there*
- *We have no way of mapping out the direction to it*

What do we want to see? What is our vision? What is that thing that we have got on our knees before God and cried out for?

My vision is very simple. It reads:

- **To make the gospel of Jesus Christ available to as many children as possible using the best possible methods and the shortest possible time**
- **To equip others to do the same**

Recently I was asked to go to Manchester to speak to a team of young people who had taken a year out to work with churches up and down the country. They were together for a couple of days and I had been asked to come and speak to them about ministry to children. I set out relatively early, giving myself enough time to get to Manchester. It was only when I was 10km outside Manchester that it dawned on me that, other than the fact that the training day was in Manchester and I was due to start speaking at 11am, I didn't know any more about the location of the training day – unfortunately this is not unusual behaviour for me!

The point I am making is this: when I set out early on that day, all I needed to know was the area where I was heading. I didn't need the detail. It was only when I was getting close to the actual area that I needed detail. Vision is not unlike this. God rarely shows us the whole picture at once. He just shows us a couple of steps so that we can start. If you are waiting for the whole picture, you will never start. You need an overview vision that as Habakkuk 2:2 says can be written down:

> *Then the LORD told me: "I will give you my message in the form of a vision. Write it clearly enough to be read at a glance."*

Your vision can be as simple as:

"I will run the largest children's club in my city."

This is not an arrogant vision, by the way. Our vision is supposed to be big. We must attempt things so amazing that, unless God steps in, we will end up flat on our faces. We must aim high.

We serve a God of creativity, who spoke and the world came into being – who took dust and "fearfully and wonderfully" formed you and me. Let's dream big dreams; let's do some amazing, exciting things for Jesus.

COMMENT

Our minds are rarely tuned in to what God is saying. Sometimes God gives us a vision and we say, "God, that is too big; how can I possibly do that?" We forget what God can do through us; we forget that we must not try to carry out God-given vision in our own strength. But equally we may get a vision from God and be tempted to say – is that it? God's ways are not our ways and sometimes our little club of 10 may have in it 10 apostles. It may seem small, but we rarely understand God's economy. The key is very simple. Listen to God and do what you're told.

An American company called General Electric has this motto:
"If we can dream it, we can do it."

Can you imagine what would happen if some people committed to the expansion of the Kingdom of God got hold of that sort of philosophy and made it part of their everyday living? NASA has an even better one:

"We are limited only by our imagination and determination and never by physics."

Let's dream some dreams. Let's make God famous.

Goals

There it is: we have begun – now we must prayerfully break it down. We need a venue; we need some people to help; we need to choose the best night, and we need some finance. We have now moved into the area of goals – the things we need to do to make the vision a reality.

At this stage we don't know which children we are going to reach; we don't know what sort of teaching we are going to use; we don't actually know if we are going to be teaching at all. Maybe it's a football club God wants us to run!

Now, as we move closer, we need more detail. Five kilometres from my destination I had to make a few frantic phone calls to find out the detail. I arrived with almost 30 seconds to spare! But at this stage the detail does become important. We need to know if it is going to be a football club. Is it a project to help Christian children? Is it an outreach project to give us the opportunity to be spiritual foster parents?

That much-used acrostic to help us set goals is the word SMART. It works as follows. Our goals must be:

Specific	What exactly are we looking to achieve – for example, to start a new club in Ourtown School Hall?
Measurable	How many people will it bring in? How many new leaders will we have?
Achievable	Can this really be done? Yes there is faith involved, but if the Seventh Day Adventists use it all week then we can't use Ourtown School Hall
Reviewable	We have said it will happen in six months; three months later it is clear it isn't going to; let's review and refocus
Time-Related	How long will it take to achieve this particular goal?

Goals allow us to work the vision out strategically. I may have a vision to run the largest children's church in my city, but it will be strategic goal-setting that will get me there. I will need to set goals: after 6 months I will have 50 children and 4 staff; after 12 months I will have 75 children and 5 leaders, etc.

Perseverance

Jesus said in Luke 9:62:

> Anyone who starts ploughing and keeps looking back isn't worth a thing to God's kingdom!

You can have the strongest burden and the most amazing vision, but if you don't have perseverance they really aren't worth much. The ability to see things through has become a lost art. So many people quit just before the miracle happens. If it was easy, it wouldn't be worth doing. It's supposed to cost us something. Let me illustrate with a narrative from 2 Chronicles 14:

> Abijah died and was buried in Jerusalem. Then his son Asa became king, and Judah had ten years of peace. Asa obeyed the LORD his God and did right. He destroyed the local shrines and the altars to foreign gods. He smashed the stone images of gods and cut down the sacred poles used in worshipping the goddess Asherah. Then he told everyone in Judah to worship the LORD God, just as their ancestors had done, and to obey his laws and teachings. He destroyed every local shrine and incense altar in

Judah. The LORD blessed Judah with peace while Asa was king, and so during that time, Asa fortified many of the towns. He said to the people, "Let's build walls and defence towers for these towns, and put in gates that can be locked with bars. This land still belongs to us, because we have obeyed the LORD our God. He has given us peace from all our enemies." The people did everything Asa had suggested.

Asa had a large army of brave soldiers: three hundred thousand of them were from the tribe of Judah and were armed with shields and spears; two hundred and eighty thousand were from Benjamin and were armed with bows and arrows.

Zerah from Ethiopia led an army of a million soldiers and three hundred chariots to the town of Mareshah in Judah. Asa met him there, and the two armies prepared for battle in Zephathah Valley.
(2 Chronicles 14:1–10)

The story starts off very positively – a righteous king who undoes the bad things his father had set in place. Asa puts God back in his rightful position and the whole nation looks well. Then, Zerah from Ethiopia decides to visit – this is not a social call; it is war. And to make life worse, Asa is in a valley – having grown up in one I'm an expert in valleys – and Asa cannot back out; if he takes his men up the mountain and out of the valley then the Ethiopians will pick them off from behind.

Vision runs the same route – it must. All starts off well, everything seems to be coming together nicely, then Zerah visits: the money runs out, a key person leaves, you hit a low attendance week, the school won't let you in any more. Zerah comes.

In this story we learn a lot about what to do when Zerah comes. Firstly it is worth noting that humanly speaking all was lost – Asa was overwhelmed and outnumbered. He wasn't being pessimistic, he was being real. He knew that he couldn't win this one in his own strength.

What an incredibly refreshing place to come to. To know that by ourselves we are lost, that by ourselves we are outnumbered and overwhelmed. It really is not wrong to end up in this position; it isn't this that decides the outcome, it's the next bit – what we do next. What our response is to the situation – not the situation itself. All the great men of God found themselves here. Paul said that in Asia he despaired even of life itself; Moses looked at a burning bush and couldn't understand why he should go; David uttered the words:

"God, if I was a dove I would fly far away from here."

Asa's responses are illuminating and noteworthy. He does two things. Firstly, he responds naturally; he does what he can do. He lines his armies up.

Our natural response might be to ask the treasurer for more money, to make an appeal for more leaders, to talk to the local council about a new hall or just to take a nap! But Asa also responds supernaturally. He prays, and in doing so he reveals to us the key – the way to make perseverance possible. He involves God in the battle. He invites God in and that makes all the difference. Asa prayed:

"God, only with you can a powerless army defeat a greater one."

He invited God in and it all changed. It always does. Paul said:

"God's power is made perfect in weakness."

Moses, although afraid, stood before Pharaoh and commanded him to let God's people go.

And of David, who wanted to fly away, Absalom the rebel comments:

"Don't go after my father now, for he is a fighter."

That's the sort of testimony we're looking for. People who persevere, people who don't give in before the job is complete, people of whom even their enemies will say that they are fighters. We must keep going and we must keep God involved, for when God is involved we become brave in danger, cheerful in monotony and positive in the face of discouragement.

Mary Shelley's story *Frankenstein* is very interesting, although the plot is very simplistic – a brilliant but mad scientist creates a person from lots of body parts and then artificially brings it to life. The person turns out to be a monster. The monster then upsets some villagers, who pursue the monster to a gothic castle, where they burn the castle and kill the monster. As well as providing generations of film makers with material, the story is also an astute insight into the futility of humanism – what happens when we leave God out of the equation and try to put together a programme by borrowing lots of components from elsewhere – we create a monster and it all ends in disaster. God must never be left out of the equation!

The outcome of the Asa story is very encouraging:

The LORD helped Asa and his army defeat the Ethiopians. The enemy soldiers ran away, but Asa and his troops chased them as far as Gerar. It was a total defeat – the Ethiopians could not even fight back! The soldiers from Judah took everything that had belonged to the Ethiopians. The people who lived in the villages around Gerar learned what had happened and were afraid of the LORD. (2 Chronicles 14:12–14)

God made us a promise:

"In this world you will have trouble."

He then attached a commandment:

"Don't be afraid, I've overcome the world."

Let's see our God-given visions through, or die trying.

CHILDREN'S WORK WASN'T LIKE THIS WHEN I WAS YOUNG!

"We didn't use to do it like this."

I've heard that a lot – an awful lot. The principle is the same for children's work as it is for every form of Christian ministry. *The message is timeless and unchanging; the style of presentation is linked to time and changes according to the culture.*

> It is not necessary that customs and forms of worship be exactly the same everywhere. Throughout history they have differed. They may be altered according to nations, times and habits of people, provided that nothing is commanded contrary to God's Word.

This – in older English – was written nearly 500 years ago by Thomas Cranmer, and forms part of the 39 Articles of Religion (Article 34).

We have to work at being relevant and learn to start from where our audience is and not from where we are. The church has spent much time criticising Philip Pullman's and J.K. Rowling's work without realising why millions of children are reading their books. Whether we like it or not, this is where the target audience is. It was sociologist Douglas Rushkoff who rightly pointed out that without moving an inch we have nonetheless travelled further than any other generation in history. This is not the generation of Enid Blyton's "Famous Five"; this is the generation of "Harry Potter".

I have defended the "Harry Potter" series diligently – not on the basis that there aren't some very concerning elements, but on the basis that we must start where this generation of children is at and work from there. Throwing verbal stones at Harry Potter only alienates the very children we want to reach. At the same time, the "Harry Potter" series gave such clear opportunities for a presentation of the gospel that I was almost grateful to Ms Rowling for writing it; we discover in *Goblet of Fire* the reason that Harry could not be hurt by Voldemort (I'm protected by an omnipotent God so I can get away with saying that name) when he was a baby. The reason was that somebody (in this case his mother) who loved him unconditionally was prepared to lay down their life for him! J.K. Rowling gives us a wonderful platform for presenting the gospel – I suspect unintentionally.

Every generation has different characteristics. And it would have been the easiest thing in the world simply to list them here. But I don't know if that would really help, so I've earthed each statement by attaching to it our response.

This Generation is Surprisingly Sophisticated

Philip Pullman and J.K. Rowling's literature is being written for and read by this generation of children. Today's children are clearly able to assimilate complex ideas, subtle plots and storylines that would not be out of place in a book for adults. Our approach to this generation must reflect this. What worked well with our 11–15s five years ago is what is working particularly well with our 8–11s now.

I was running the children's ministry for those aged 8–11 at a large conference recently. That particular evening, after the children's session had finished and the main celebrations were done, there was to be a concert by The Tribe (a very popular dance/R&B band) geared to the teenagers. I stood at the back to see what the concert was like and there filling the front rows were 90% of the children who had only hours earlier been in the children's meeting. They were dancing, and, more interestingly, they knew the words to nearly every song.

Our Response

The whole thing is moving forward at an alarming pace and to keep relevant we have to immerse ourselves in the culture. That isn't as hard as it sounds. It simply means that we have to spend time with children, listen to the way they speak, look at the games they play, watch the programmes they watch, buy the music they are buying. We must continually update the work we do with children or very soon we will discover that we are no longer relevant and have drifted back into babysitting.

This is a Very Discerning Generation

If there has been a "disagreement" between two members of staff just before you open the doors to your children's club, the children will know. They don't need to be told, they don't need to have overheard, they will not be able to explain how they know, but they *will* know. What's more it will affect them. The manipulative members of the group will work hard at keeping the disagreement alive and will pour as much salt on the wound as possible. The sensitive children will feel upset and become tearful. The more rowdy children will become even rowdier. You are not in for a good evening.

Our Response

The atmosphere the children walk into must be calm and peaceful. Some of these children are attending in order to escape the civil war they face in their homes on a regular basis; there is no place for war within the children's club.

We must be a godly example as well as teach godly principles. What we are and what we say must never be contradictory.

● This Generation has No Respect for Authority

As in most of these areas, if we can take our lead from Jesus then we can't go far wrong. Jesus could have presented the Sermon on the Mount like this. He could have asked one of his disciples to go on first and warm the crowd up and then the disciple could introduce Jesus.

"Ladies and gentlemen, for one night only, for your entertainment: the King of Kings, the Prince of Peace, The Son of God, yes… Here's Jesus."

And then some angels would appear and blow trumpets and Jesus would descend on a cloud wearing his best white outfit and present the Sermon on the Mount.

He could have. But he didn't. He stood as he was; he didn't make any claims. He simply stood and talked. He didn't hide behind his authority, and as a result the ordinary people flocked to hear him.

Our Response

In the words of Sting (he's a singer, not a book in the Bible):

"Be yourself no matter what they say."

We never need to hide behind titles. One day the King of the Universe decided to adopt us as his son/daughter; he chose us; he reconciled us; he appointed us. We are princes/princesses. We don't need to continually restate it; we just *are* it. When we walk into spiritual darkness the light within us dispels it even before we begin to speak. We are these things; we don't need to struggle or strive for prominence or position. How much higher could we get? So when we enter a school or a children's club or a conference we stand tall – Psalm 3:3 tells me that God is the glory and the lifter of my head. So we can stand tall and confident in who we are, with no need for titles.

● Total Media Exposure

Children today are exposed to all the great issues of life from a very early age: war, crime, sex, violence – they sit and digest it all on TV. They are bombarded with information at an alarming rate. I overheard my daughter recently talking to her friend. My daughter asked:

"Have you logged on to the CBBC website yet?"

The friend responded:

"Of course I have."

Both little girls were still in reception class! They had been checking out the latest information on the Children's BBC website. The problem is this: knowledge does not equal wisdom. Children have a huge amount of information but don't know what to do with it, or, more seriously, don't have the understanding to use that knowledge properly. In the Bible knowledge equals responsibility and responsibility denied brings guilt. Add to this the fact that children are now maturing earlier and we have an insight into the potential nightmare. Children becoming pregnant before they reach their teenage years: they know about the mechanics; they have knowledge, but no understanding of the consequences. Total media exposure is a time bomb waiting to explode. So far I suspect we have only seen a few hand grenades going off.

Our Response

You will see in the chapters on programme construction that I advocate a fun item called "Buy it or Bin it". It is a time when the children are allowed to listen to music that they would normally listen to, or watch a video clip of their favourite programmes or movies and then a panel is asked whether they would buy the music/movie or whether they would bin it. They are then asked why. They are not allowed to get away with "Because I don't like it." They must quantify their response a little better than that. "Buy it or Bin it" and items like it are more than fun items; they stimulate the children to develop something called "critical thought". The ability not to allow tons of information to pour in, but to sift it, to analyse it, to evaluate it. With our own children we mustn't just switch channels when a bad programme comes on – we need to allow our children to understand why it isn't good for them to watch. When you watch adverts with your children, don't simply allow them to wash over you; talk about why the advert is good or bad.

All these things aid in the development of critical thought. Children are naturally sponge-like and will absorb anything. Guide them into a place of conscious choice with understanding. We are not just in the business of teaching; we are in the business of teaching them how to respond.

● Very Superficial

Perhaps we can better designate this as the child's ability to become all things to all people. In the children's club they can answer the questions, sing the songs, and behave like an angel. With their mates they can resort to a whole new vocabulary involving words that you didn't think they knew. They can be wild, or have no respect for property; they can be basically sinful. And sometimes if we could see these children in these various settings outside the children's club we would be horrified at the apparent deception taking place.

This is a superficial generation. George Whitfield said, "God cannot pour out his Spirit on a superficial generation."

Our Response

I genuinely wish there was a shortcut here. But there isn't. What we mustn't do is question the fact that they have made a genuine decision to be a Christian simply because we see them behaving in a less than saintly manner elsewhere. Salvation may be instantaneous; sanctification certainly is not. Without feeling discouraged we simply keep doing what we do. We teach the truth because we know that ultimately it will overwhelm the lies. We keep on training the children in the way that they should go.

● The Deterioration of the Family as a Stable Base of Support

I currently spend some time each month on the family panel at the local magistrates' court and listen to stories that simply horrify me. Before me will be sat one woman and many men, with a tribe of children involved – it will invariably be regarding custody of a particular child. But without DNA testing it is impossible to know which father belongs to which child. The frightening thing is that the mother doesn't know either.

There is one particular address on a previous children's club register; five children attended from that address, and every single one of them had a different surname. The same mum – mum had actually been married to some of the dads but no two children had the same dad. It may be an extreme example, but it is probably similar to what you see on your registers.

Our Response

We shouldn't be judgemental or jump to the conclusion that it's a chaotic home. In the above example, mum is one of the nicest people you could ever hope to meet. She genuinely loves her children even though she is unsure who their fathers are; the children are always clean and tidy, the home is immaculately tidy, and, for the number of children in it, remarkably calm. In regard to her children she is a very together mother; her children are doing well in school. She needs Jesus, but so do a lot of people. *It is not our place to judge people; it is our place to love people.* You may have children who attend your club whose parents are homosexual or bisexual or dad may be in prison. We now have a child attending our activities who is in the care of lesbian foster parents – I am not sure what you would make of that, but it was either that or stay with a father who would probably kill him. Let me repeat: it is not our place to judge; it is our place to love. Some children may be drawing their sense of peace and security from your club – glory to God, that's why we're there. Some children may be looking to us as a father or mother figure – great, be a good example.

● An Increase in Stress and Anxiety along with a Decrease in Hope and Joy

Ever heard a seven-year-old utter the sentence: "Leave me alone, I'm stressed"? I have, with increasing frequency. I am a fanatical supporter of the child's right to be a child. I think the United Nations' Convention on the Rights of the Child is a marvellous document. It underlines the child's right to be a child – to feel safe and secure in doing dumb things, to laugh and play and love. In my previous church one of our team returned from a missionary trip to the Balkans and told me of an incident that happened on the Albania/Macedonia border. He told me that there were soldiers everywhere, missiles going off, guns being fired, flashes in the sky. And only 100 metres from the war zone there was a group of about 20 children who had managed to get hold of a football from one of the soldiers, and they were having the time of their lives. Bombs exploding, warfare taking place and in the middle children playing. What a message of hope! *The child's ability to find life and hope and joy and laughter in the midst of war has never ceased to amaze me.* Abused children, hurt children, damaged children can come through with the ability to laugh and play. We serve a great God who restores lives.

Our Response

Yes, our clubs must be places where the gospel is proclaimed. Yes, the decisions the children make there are life-and-death, heaven-or-hell decisions, but please let them also be places of fun and joy.

● No Cohesive Meta-narrative

While taking part recently in a Christian conference, I was staying at an hotel overnight. I arrived back late one night and I was more than a little surprised to see gentlemen rushing around in dinner suits followed closely by ladies in low-cut black dresses. I was a little concerned and was beginning to think I had entered the twilight zone. The truth turned out to be equally bizarre: the hotel I was staying at was staging a "James Bond" theme night! This was a cohesive meta-narrative. A group of people from a diversity of backgrounds with something in common.

By "meta-narrative", we simply mean the common thread that connects people and forms them into communities rather than simply collections of individuals. I grew up in a Welsh valley where everyone knew everyone else. Not only did they know you, they also knew your father and grandfather. At some point the whole valley had a common thread – the coal pit. Most of my friends' grandfathers had worked at it or in trades related to it. The valley still maintained its meta-narratives. Small villages still to some extent hold on to their meta-narrative and hence it is difficult for people to move into the community. However, this is becoming more and more rare, and it takes very special events to give people a cohesive meta-narrative.

In recent history the death of Diana, Princess of Wales was one such occasion. Millions of people nationally and internationally were fused into communities with a common meta-narrative – in this case their feelings of grief and loss.

Unfortunately, the experience was short-lived and people quickly drifted back to being collections of individuals again. It is a fact that more and more people are leaving villages all over the world and being drawn to large cities – huge people-centres. The interesting thing is that people are now living more closely together than at any other point in history, yet they feel more isolated and alone than at any other point of history.

Our Response

The church has a major role to play in this whole area. For generations the parish church existed as more than a place of worship; it existed as the place where the community came together. The place where relationships were formed. The place where children experienced what it is to have a wider family: a wider family that provided support and care for the actual family. Through our wider activities, our community events, our all-age worship, we can reintroduce that common meta-narrative. A community loving God and loving one another. Sound idealistic? Then let's work towards the ideal.

● An Erosion of Moral Absolutes

Society seems to do some strange things. In the last decade Holland legalised many hard drugs and then boasted to the rest of Europe that it had halved the number of convictions for drug offences. The amazing thing is that very few people saw the ridiculousness of the statement. The drug use hadn't changed; all that had changed was that it was now legally allowed. We could take the label off the bottle of poison and relabel it as orange juice; it wouldn't change the fact that you would die if you drank it.

Society seems very cautious about saying some things are right and some things are wrong. One nursery school recently featured in the newspapers because, on the advice of the local council, it refused to tell children they were being naughty; they feared that it would somehow restrict their development.

What one generation tolerates, the next generation accepts. We are in danger of living in an age where the maxim becomes: "do what you want as long as you don't hurt anyone". If we say something is evil or wrong then society says *we* are evil!

Our Response

Our children's club must have non-negotiable rules:

"When the whistle blows, everyone is silent."

"If you get three warnings in free play then you are banned for a week."

Do the rules inhibit? Do they restrict enjoyment? Absolutely not! It is much more difficult to have fun in chaos than it is in organised activity. Children feel safe knowing where the boundaries are. From time to time they will test the boundary by deliberately breaking the rule. You must enforce the rule at this point. It will help them feel more secure. Even if it means they are banned for a week, they will come back. They always do, and this time they are more secure in the boundary.

Underlying the whole of the above must be a heartfelt understanding that truth will always overcome lies, life will always overcome death and, 2,000 years on, John's statement still holds true:

The light shines in the darkness, and the darkness can never extinguish it, comprehend it or even understand it. (John 1:5, Amplified Version)

LEARNING A NEW LANGUAGE

A man once said: "He who learns to communicate to a generation ultimately has the power to control that generation."

And while we need to be very clear that for us it is not about control (control is something the devil wants to do to people, but it violates one of God's greatest gifts to us, free will), we do need to influence the generation. And to influence this generation for godliness and righteousness involves communicating well. After all, if God has called us to do children's work then our very vocation is communication. He has gifted us and sent us to communicate the good news about his Kingdom and about a God who loves unconditionally.

When we want to chop a tree down, there is very little point in hitting the tree harder and harder if the axe itself is blunt. What we need to do is sharpen the axe.

On a recent visit to a restaurant in France it was interesting to watch a particularly arrogant Englishman trying to order his food. He clearly had no knowledge of French, and the waitress for her part had very little knowledge of English. The man wanted chips with his meal instead of the potatoes that came as standard. He asked the waitress repeatedly for "chips", and when she continued to look blankly at him he began to shout the word "chips" at her very loudly. The waitress, instead of suddenly realising what the man wanted because he was now shouting louder, was now looking around desperately for a policeman to rescue her from the mad Englishman.

I am unsure where the idea came from, but somewhere locked away in our psyche is a theory that says that if we are not being understood then we need to raise the volume. Many of us may have experienced similar events in our churches: when the preacher sees blank faces staring back at him he begins to shout his message in an attempt to be understood! Unfortunately, it doesn't work. If we would like to be understood then we need to speak in a language that is understandable and not simply raise the volume – this will have exactly the opposite effect.

When it comes to communication with children the goal must surely not be harder and louder, but sharper and clearer. To be able to influence this generation we must be understood; we must communicate well. But before we jump in, allow me to interject the warning:

I say only what the Father who sent me has told me to say, in the way that he has told me to say it. (John 12:49)

Clearly, Jesus is our best example of a great communicator, but he is telling us that he only speaks what the Father has told him to, in the way the Father has told him.

So two clear points can be drawn from this verse:

1.   The Father tells us what to say
2.   The Father tells us how to say it

So the Father gives us the message and, just as important, he also gives us the method of delivery. With that in mind, let's move on.

Here is the format for the first fifteen minutes of a particular episode of *Sesame Street*:

1.   Elmo going to meet Prince Charming
2.   Titles
3.   Elmo meets Prince but he's on the cellular phone
4.   Elmo meets Prince but he's on the fax
5.   Elmo meets Prince but he's on the normal phone
6.   Elmo meets Prince but he's on the answerphone
7.   Prince Charming is stressed and resigns
8.   Video – telephone ringing in street
9.   Animation – talking walking telephone
10. Video – two children make a map of neighbourhood and then explain their map
11. Animation – the letter K: kangaroo, kite, etc
12. Video – the city garden project
13. Puppets – dance and rap
14. Humans chatting about poems
15. Interview – Big Bird meets a poet: what is a poem, a game with words
16. Animation – toothpaste
17. Video – how to clean your teeth
18. Animation – I love my teeth
19. Song – toothbrush song

Nineteen different components in only fifteen minutes of television. The longest item was the title sequence itself. *Sesame Street* is aimed at a pre-school audience. And then we come to our children's club and we have prepared well. We have an excellent story, an excellent talk, an excellent object lesson, but the children don't seem interested; they are fidgety, they whisper to each other, they pull each other's hair. We think we have failed, but it's not us. We think they are rude and just plain naughty, but it's not them. From pre-school onwards this generation has learnt to digest information in small pieces, presented in different ways and presented very quickly. They would love to listen to your story, they would love to give you their full attention, but since pre-school they have been taught to enjoy a fast-moving, constantly changing programme; they would love to listen, but they don't know how.

I visited a school recently while it was undergoing a week-long inspection (I am invited in to take assemblies at many schools when the inspectors are visiting – I am beginning to suspect it is no coincidence). I took the assembly and talked to the 300 children from age four to eight who attend the school. I managed to have a quick conversation with one of the inspectors at the end, and asked how the school was doing. Her response was revealing. She told me that, as in most schools up and down the country, the children were struggling to sit still for more than five minutes.

This is an entertainment-based culture. Today's children enjoy being involved, and love experimenting, but they need their information in bite-sized parcels.

The part the inspector was struggling with was how I had managed to hold 300 children's attention for 25 minutes by just standing at the front and talking. I smiled and told her that I practised a lot. The truth is, I know a secret. I know how this generation digests information. *I know that to be listened to you have to present a spiritual diet conaining all the essential food groups, but package it so that it looks like a Big Mac™*. I told a story and into that story I wove other stories, and I said the same thing in several ways.

There are two fundamental systems of communication:

1. Deductive communication

This is based on linear logic and is the type primarily taught by our theological colleges. It usually involves an introduction, three points and a conclusion. If I were to talk about "love" using this type of communication, then I would do it as follows:

- Introduction   Today I am going to talk about love and I will touch on three Greek words associated with it.
- Part 1   Phileo love
- Part 2   Eros love
- Part 3   Agape love
- Conclusion   Today we talked about love and the three Greek words associated with it.

The problem with this is simple. As soon as children know the ending they no longer feel the need to listen, so as soon as they discover that there are three Greek words for love from the introduction, they no longer feel the need to listen, and they don't.

2. Inductive communication

Induction is entertainment-based. In this method people are drawn into the presentation and don't know where the end is until it arrives. If we were to show a structure it would look something like this:

Attention	...	Grab the audience's attention (if this doesn't happen in the first 30 seconds it is not going to happen)
Interest	...	Keep the audience interested
Conviction	...	Draw the audience to the conclusion, showing them how it applies to them
Response	...	Never let the audience go without giving them the opportunity to respond in one way or another

If I were to talk about "love" using this method of communication, I might start like this...

> *A man was travelling from Jerusalem to Jericho when he fell into the hands of thieves and robbers...* (Luke 10:30)

Jesus, the master communicator, communicated inductively. Our theological colleges rarely list Jesus as a great preacher. He doesn't fit the modern preaching paradigm. Yet he was an amazing communicator whom the people of the day would travel for miles to hear. And he could hold the attention of all ages at the same time and in the same place. However, when we look at his style and technique, we soon discover that *Sesame Street* isn't so original after all. Jesus' Sermon on the Mount was approximately 18 minutes long, yet into that 18 minutes Jesus packed 348 different images and experiences from everyday life. 221 times he says "YOU" as opposed to "some people", and he uses comedy.

We must learn to let our programmes evolve, but understand the need for fast-moving, magazine-style content. We must have the confidence to try different things and not be overly concerned if they fail dismally. Out of ten programme items, only five may work. That is not a problem: when we start the following week we know we have five items that work well. We must never be afraid of making mistakes, for, as one entrepreneur put it, "if we don't make mistakes, we'll never make anything". We should never be afraid of making mistakes; we should fear only the absence of creative, constructive and corrective responses to those mistakes. If you talk to any experienced children's worker they will be able to list a whole catalogue of mistakes that they have made as they travelled on their journey from average to expert. Remember, experts are hewn out of the bedrock of experience, and it's rare that all experiences are positive.

Having spent some time talking about the method of presenting the message, it is important to state that it really doesn't matter at the end of the day how good the method of presentation is or how good the message is, if the messenger is somehow flawed. We think our battle is in the area of apologetics – *what* we say. It's not. ***Children are not so much interested in what we say as in who we are.*** The statistics speak for themselves.

When we communicate: *15% of our message is to do with content*
25% of our message is to do with tone
60% of our message is to do with who we are

When I stand in front of a group of children and speak, my message amounts to only 15% of my overall communication. If my tone is not consistent with my message – for example, if I tell the children that God loves them but my tone is sarcastic – then the 25% overrides the 15% and I will not communicate anything other than sarcasm. The next stage is, if I tell the children that God loves them and my tone agrees with my message, but in my heart I am wishing I was at home in my cosy house watching television, then who I am overrides my tone and message and again I communicate nothing. To put all this another way, we could draw on the Zulu proverb:

"I can't hear what you are saying because who you are is shouting in my face."

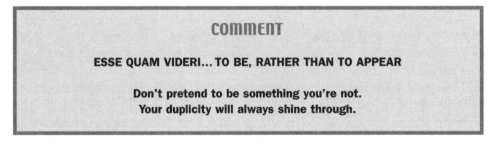

COMMENT

ESSE QUAM VIDERI... TO BE, RATHER THAN TO APPEAR

**Don't pretend to be something you're not.
Your duplicity will always shine through.**

There are three basics that we need to know. The problem is, they are so basic that most people overlook how important they actually are:

1. If the children don't like you, they will not listen to you

We all know this to be true. When we were in school – however long ago it may have been – we learnt the most from the teachers we liked and the least from the teachers we didn't. It's just one of those facts of life; we learn from those we like and particularly when we think they like us. If the children don't like you, then it really is all over. They will not listen.

2. If you will not have fun with them, they will not listen to you

Children will always listen to someone who has taken the time to have fun with them, to get down to their level, to play their games. Those who have taken an interest in the children's world will always have an advantage.

3. If you will not listen to them, they will not listen to you

Any children's worker who has been doing the work for any significant period of time will have a story about how they were on the brink of a cliff-hanger ending to their best story when a little boy or girl shouted out:

"I went to the supermarket today and I bought yoghurt."

Nothing to do with the story, but this child has waited all day long to tell the story of their adventure at the supermarket and, as they hadn't had an opportunity before, this seems to be a great opportunity, when everyone else is quiet. We only have ourselves to blame. If at any point in the programme we had given the child a chance to talk, then we could have finished our amazing story. What's worse is when the child interrupts your story with something far more serious:

"My mum and dad are arguing all the time."

But the cause is the same. They were not allowed time to express themselves earlier on.

In my view these three things are "basic basics" and 99% of the readers of this book will agree. But how many people actually design their programmes to take these things into consideration? *How many people design their programmes so that children can have fun with them, so that children can talk to them, so that children can get to like them?* The answer is a lot fewer than 99%.

If these things are important, then when the children arrive give them time to sit in a café area and eat chocolate, to play on some computers, or to bounce a ball outside with you before the teaching programme kicks off. They can share their adventures at the supermarket or their more serious concerns about life at home in the café area; they can have fun with you as they destroy you yet again on the computer games and on the basketball court and they can just hang out with you and get to know you – and, more importantly, to like you. We need some children's workers out there who are absolute heroes to their children's group. It is hard to underestimate the importance of play. The United Nations Convention on the Rights of the Child states that children have the right to play! Play allows us opportunity to mix with the children, to learn from the children, to win the right to speak into their lives.

WARNING

You will be tempted to fill your programme with videos and music and all sorts of technological wonders in an attempt to reach this technologically-advanced generation. Never lose sight of the fact that the technology does not have a heart. And spectacular though your presentation may be, our greatest communication will always come from our heart. This is why the man or woman who communicates from their heart will always communicate more effectively than the man or woman who relies on PowerPoint™ or some other multimedia device. Use technology to add to your presentation – never make the technology the presentation itself.

Having talked about preparation of the message and preparation of the messenger, allow me to touch on my pet passion to end this chapter. We need to be right; we need to communicate well, but we must never lose sight of the fact that God has called us to preach, to proclaim his word. To do it with passion and integrity, with compassion and power. Ultimately when we talk to children we are preaching a timeless message that changes lives, communities, cities and worlds. *A message that did and will again rock nations; proclamation that will sometimes bypass the head and speak directly into hearts.* The need of the day is children's workers who are full of the Holy Spirit, who will proclaim, in a relevant and contemporary manner, the message of the cross and the principles of God's word. **Don't tell cute stories – change lives.**

SALVATION AND OTHER GIFTS FROM GOD

Pointing a child to Christ and giving them a clear opportunity to respond to the gospel message is plainly one of the most important parts of our work with children. Allowing children to praise Jesus and to be able to hear from God themselves is a wonderful sign of their developing spiritual maturity, and is very rewarding for children's workers to see. But how do these things work in practice?

Being a children's worker can be very encouraging, and in large groups you can usually report that at least ten children have responded to the gospel message every month. However, it usually transpires that they are the same ten children every time. Some children will raise their hands to become a Christian just because their friends do; some children will raise their hands to become a Christian simply because they know it will please you. Others may respond very positively and you will be convinced that they have met with God, but on your way out of the building you may see them with their friends engaged in activities and using words that make you doubt their salvation experience!

Whatever the reasons, it is clear that it is always safer for us to report "Ten children responded to the gospel message tonight," rather than to say, "Ten children became Christians tonight."

COMMENT

It is worthwhile pointing out here that raising your hand is only one of many ways of indicating a desire to become a Christian – children may be encouraged to kneel, to stand, or to respond by placing a list of things they feel they have done wrong into a bin, to show repentance and forgiveness. It is perfectly acceptable to be creative. When all is said and done, it is the change of heart that is important; the physical response is simply a way of expressing that change of heart.

Does that mean that children are not making genuine decisions for Christ? Not at all: in fact, statistically speaking, 80% of the present church population made their decision to become a Christian before the age of fourteen, and the vast majority of that 80% made their decision before the age of twelve. So is it wrong to make appeals? Again, I don't think so. If nothing else, the children's response shows that they are interested in knowing more about God. And in actuality how much more can we discern from an adult making a similar decision? The response shows us at least that the person responding may want to know more.

What do we do when a child responds? It is clear that they need to hear a little more about the gospel. Allow those who have responded to meet together with a leader who can present the gospel message in more depth. DO NOT TAKE THE CHILDREN TO A DIFFERENT ROOM. Parents turning up early to collect their child will feel very uncomfortable if he or she has been taken away from the main group. Talk to those who have responded in the same hall or room as the rest of the children, no matter how difficult this may prove.

And once they are in the smaller group, what do they need to hear about the gospel? In order for us to explain the gospel adequately to children we need a clear understanding of three areas BEFORE we can start. We need to know about:

1. God
2. The children
3. Jesus

I'll explain the theology behind these three areas, but in reality the illustration in the Appendix and the smaller version opposite will aid the process. Other organisations produce excellent booklets that communicate the gospel message, but it is imperative that the items listed opposite are covered:

1. God

a. God is **LOVE** – **"God is love. If we keep on loving others, we will stay united in our hearts with God, and he will stay united with us."** (1 John 4:16)
b. God is absolutely **PURE** – **"That's why the Scriptures say, 'I am the holy God, and you must be holy too'."** (1 Peter 1:16)
c. God is **FAIR** – **"It is only right for God to punish everyone who is causing you trouble."** (2 Thessalonians 1:6)

2. The Children

a. We were created good, but became **SINFUL**. Sin is the rubbish, the junk and the garbage in our lives, the wrong things we do – **"All of us have sinned and fallen short of God's glory."** (Romans 3:23)

LEADING A CHILD TO CHRIST	
GOD	**YOU**
God is **LOVE** – 1 John 4:16 God is **FAIR** – 2 Thessalonians 1:6 God is absolutely **PURE** – 1 Peter 1:16	We were created good, but became **SINFUL** – Romans 3:23 We deserve to be **PUNISHED** for doing wrong things – Romans 6:23 There is **NOTHING WE CAN DO** to fix it – Isaiah 64:6
JESUS	**RESPONSE**
JESUS is **GOD**, who also became man – John 1:14 Christ died as our **SUBSTITUTE** – 1 Peter 2:24 Christ offers his forgiveness as a **FREE GIFT** – Ephesians 2:8–9	You and I must **RESPOND** – Romans 10:13 We must ask Christ to be our **FORGIVER AND LEADER** – 1 John 1:9

b. We deserve to be **PUNISHED** for doing wrong things – **"Sin pays off with death. But God's gift is eternal life given by Jesus Christ our Lord."** (Romans 6:23)

3. Jesus

a. JESUS is GOD, who also became man – **"In the beginning was the one who is called the Word. The Word was with God and was truly God... The Word became a human being and lived here with us. We saw his true glory, the glory of the only Son of the Father. From him all the kindness and all the truth of God have come down to us."** (John 1:14)

b. Christ died as our **SUBSTITUTE** – **"Christ carried the burden of our sins. He was nailed to the cross, so that we would stop sinning and start living right. By his cuts and bruises you are healed."** (1 Peter 2:24)
   c. Christ offers his forgiveness as a **FREE GIFT** – **"You were saved by faith in God, who treats us much better than we deserve. This is God's gift to you, and not anything you have done on your own. It isn't something you have earned, so there is nothing you can boast about."** (Ephesians 2:8–9)

And after talking the children through the above (or at least a summary of the above), we can give them an opportunity to respond again:

   a. You and I must **RESPOND** – **"Yet some people accepted him and put their faith in him. So he gave them the right to be the children of God."** (John 1:12)
   b. We must ask Christ to be our **FORGIVER AND LEADER** – **"But if we confess our sins to God, he can always be trusted to forgive us and take our sins away."** (1 John 1:9)

At this point, say a prayer with the children that they can repeat, asking God to become their forgiver and leader.

   c. The result is that **GOD TAKES AWAY OUR SIN AND BECOMES PART OF OUR LIVES** – **"Anyone who belongs to Christ is a new person. The past is forgotten, and everything is new."** (2 Corinthians 5:17)

Having completed this process, invite the children to promise to do two things before they go to sleep that night:

   1. They will pray the prayer asking God to become their leader and forgiver one more time in their own words
   2. They will tell someone they can trust what they have done

What about hearing from God and spiritual gifts?

   I intend only to give a brief overview of this area. For further help, might I suggest that you read David Pytches' excellent book *Come Holy Spirit*, with an understanding that all the items listed (including the Baptism in the Holy Spirit) are available to children.

   It is important that children see an example of spiritual gifts in operation in adults. Just because it is a children's gathering does not mean that God doesn't want adults to use spiritual gifts. It is wonderful to be a children's leader when another leader has just used a spiritual gift, to simply be able to say:

"That's what we call the gift of prophecy. God says that you don't have to be an adult to do that; it simply involves hearing from God and telling others what he said."

People being obedient to God is the best object lesson we will ever present.

I prefer to give the children an opportunity to share what God has been saying to them at the end of, or sometimes during, the quieter songs. Elisha in 2 Kings 3:15 asks for a musician to come so he can listen to God and proclaim his word. This is the biblical basis, but at the end of the day it boils down to style and personal preference. I have no doubt that children could listen to God and share what he is saying in total silence. It really doesn't matter; what *does* matter is that children are given the opportunity to hear from God, and very often God will give them something to share with the group.

In practice, at the end of a quieter song I would explain to the children that not only does God want us to talk to him, but he also wants to talk to *us*. I explain that sometimes God speaks to us and what God says may be just for us. God may want to whisper into our hearts that he is always with us. However, there are times when God speaks to us and the words he whispers into our hearts are for us to share with others. He may want us to tell them all that he loves everyone, no matter what they have done. Sometimes he may show us a picture of something and tell us the meaning of the picture. Make it very clear that to the children that they are in a safe environment and nobody will laugh if they get it wrong.

Some of the words that children have shared in these times have blown me away. Sometimes they have a depth and maturity that is far beyond what I would expect. Sometimes they are just very amusing. But God really does love to get involved in young lives. Children have seen maps of countries that God wants them to go to when they are older; children have told other children that they don't need to be afraid any more because God will protect them, and others have burst into tears as the strength of the message has hit them. 80% of our missionaries heard God calling them to the mission field as children.

I ask the children to share whatever God is telling them with another leader first before I allow them to announce it to the group. This means that we don't allow a child to embarrass themselves or for that matter to share something that God is speaking clearly and personally to *them* about.

Some churches would call this the gift of prophecy; others would call it seeing visions: for my part I am not particularly interested in the terminology – it is simply very exciting to see children touching God and touching the supernatural.

A final warning to end the chapter: beware of too much emotion. It can be counter-productive. Children can get worked up very quickly; they can get very emotional very quickly. It is your responsibility to keep it God-centred. It's not easy, but it is important.

PUTTING IT ALL TOGETHER

Reaching children is not enough. We must do much more than plant and harvest; we need to look after God's crop. Allow me to change metaphors: the lambs need a shepherd and the lambs will not be lambs for ever.

So several children have given their lives to Jesus (as discussed in an earlier chapter). Many of them are very keen to know more about Jesus; they want to grow in Christ. What is the best way to disciple these children?

The centre circle represents our leaders and **developing leaders** – (see chapter on developing leaders).

The next circle out is where our discipleship takes place in **small groups**.

The outer circle is for our **large gatherings**; this is where we see children won for Jesus and basic Bible teaching take place.

The section on starting from scratch gives insight into the "whens" and the "hows"; here we are simply looking at the "why".

Large Gatherings

Into this circle we could place our outreach children's club that exists for the primary reason of winning boys and girls for Jesus, and also our children's church/Sunday school group that exists for the children of church families. You may not have structured your programme like this, and it really doesn't matter, but what I am trying to communicate is the idea that there is an outer group which contains the majority of children that we teach and speak to on a regular basis.

This is our big pool, from which we draw those who will continue on to more meaningful and strategic discipleship.

How do we choose those who should join our small groups? Basically we want to take as many as possible (and as many as small-group leaders allow) from our large gatherings and into smaller groups. But small groups are for those who have an interest in knowing more about God and who have made a serious commitment to Christ or are at least seriously interested.

Summer camps also allow us to get to know many children better and to invite them to join our small-group activities.

I am a great believer in summer camps. I know that many churches don't run summer camps or provide opportunities for their children to attend such camps. Let me try to persuade you of the benefits of attending such camps as a group.

Possibly before we do that I should define what we mean by summer camps for children. The children from the local church children's club go to an organised activity and spiritual input week – only the older children (8–12s) are allowed to attend. The local church or camp organisers will ensure that there is one leader for every six children who attend. The camps are usually held at public schools with dormitory accommodation. The camp will have an activity director and someone responsible for spiritual input throughout the week. The format of each day will usually follow a similar routine, mixing Bible study and physical and craft-based activities.

With groups attending from all over the country, the children have an excellent opportunity to make friendships with children their own age and to gain a whole pile of new pen-friends. There are also advantages in taking your group to your own camp. This can be a much smaller-scale affair but will provide a great opportunity to get to know your children better. It will also mean that you can gear the activities and Bible studies very specifically. With ministry from experienced children's ministers you know that the children will be presented with a dynamic picture of God – a God who wants to be involved in their lives; a God who maybe wants to do some healing of past hurts and a God who has a glorious and victorious future for them.

As well as this, the camp also gives the leaders a wonderful opportunity to get to know their children better. To play sport with them, to prayer-walk with them, to spend time chatting at the barbecue with them, to pray with them.

DAILY CAMP PROGRAMME

7:30am	... Staff and Leaders meet for prayer
8:15am	... Children's Prayer Walk
9:00am	... Breakfast
10:00am	... Children's Bible Study
11:00am	... Morning Activities (swimming, games, video)
1:30pm	... Lunch
3:00pm	... Afternoon Activities (tournaments, assault course, workshops)
5:30pm	... Dinner
7:00pm	... Celebration for all with music and preaching
9:00pm	... Supper
9:30pm	... Children meet with their party leaders for feedback and prayer
10:00pm	... Lights Out
10:15pm	... Staff and Party Leaders' Chill Out

Those children who attend children's camp should all be given the opportunity to become part of a small discipleship group on their return; a chance to continue their walk with God and a chance to earth some of the things they have experienced in the spiritually, and often emotionally, charged environment of camp.

Summer camps provide the opportunity for God to change children's lives, and – just as exciting – I have seen many leaders renew their passion for children's ministry in these weeks. Everyone leaves with a clear understanding that their body needs some time for recovery but their spirit is strong!

If you've never been to summer camp I've included a useful contact address in the resource section.

COMMENT

Bible Weeks such as New Wine and Spring Harvest also allow time for the children to experience a series of powerful children's meetings that facilitate times of significant spiritual growth, without the need for the vast organisation of taking children to summer camps – the downside, of course, is that children who do not have Christian parents are rarely taken to Bible Weeks.

Small Groups

At this level the children are split into small groups. The word "choose" is very important here: children cannot be made to move into this circle. The children here choose to learn more. They have a desire to discover more about God. They are a pleasure to teach because they are hungry for spiritual things.

COMMENT

When a child joins a small group they should still be encouraged to attend the large gatherings. They need both, and ultimately when we incorporate them into our leadership groups we should encourage them to attend large gatherings, small groups and leadership groups. All three groups are important and cater for different areas.

The teaching may take place in the church, or in a home, or in the park. There are child-protection issues which may make the church the best option, but the location isn't the main thing as long as it is suitable for discipleship. What *is* important is that it really is a small group. There should never be more than twelve. *The classes are for discipleship, which means teaching and praying and playing together.* Make sure the group has plenty of outings and fun activities as well as Bible study. The groups should be led by two adults, to be consistent with your child-protection policies.

The groups should meet on a regular basis – every week during term-time is a useful pattern – and should cover themes such as: Sin, Salvation, Faith, Jesus as Forgiver, Jesus as Leader, Eucharist, What is Church, Spending Time with God, Fruits of Repentance, Baptism, Bible Construction, Reading and Study, Prayer, Worship, Giving, Friends, Trusting God, Growing in God, Obeying God, Serving Others, Sacrifice, Temperament, Gifts of God, You have a Ministry, Developing Daily Devotions, Telling Others about Jesus, Missions.

Here is a possible pattern for your small groups:

> Week 1 Teaching Night
> 2 Children Teach*
> 3 Teaching Night
> 4 Fun Night

Run the small groups like home groups for children. Allow children to be added at any point, but when the group exceeds twelve then split it into two.

Remember this is children's discipleship. If they start these groups when they are eight they will only be with you for three to four years before they move to youth discipleship, which is a whole new arena. It should be the goal of every children's department to pass on to their youth department young people who are full of God, who know how to read and pray, who know the importance of service and who want to see the Kingdom of God extended.

Leaders

Leadership development happens here. The chapter on leadership discusses this further, but at this point we are talking about children in leadership positions: children operating our PA systems; children welcoming others as they arrive; children speaking at our Bible studies; children speaking in our large children's gatherings; children under close supervision speaking in our adult meetings; children in charge of giving out the Bibles; children welcoming other children on Sunday mornings.

My friend Louise Davies, who heads up a large children's ministry in Sheffield, pointed out:

---

* Talk for a couple of minutes on a verse they have read that week.

We used to say that children were tomorrow's church; we have now almost universally dumped this idea and adopted the saying that children are today's church and tomorrow's leaders. But nowhere in the Bible does it say that you have to be a certain age to be a leader.

This group spends most of its time in the SMALL GROUP discipleship area, but is drawn out to experience leadership. They are unlikely to be ministering on the Billy Graham level, but it is important that they have a chance to experience a level of responsibility, an opportunity to feel what it is like to be in charge.

TIP

It is important to give your children in the leadership circle a chance to experience leadership in various contexts. Invite yourselves to other clubs and allow your young leaders to run the programme. Also look into sending them on short-term missions with organisations such as Youth With A Mission's King's Kids. King's Kids give leadership opportunities for children through to younger teens. Their website address is in "Recommended Resources".

The Youth Link

If you are a parent then you will know that children grow at a staggering rate. Before you know it, they are all grown up. Something similar happens to children's leaders. It feels as if children have only just arrived, and suddenly they are old enough to move into the youth programme.

There is a nationally identifiable problem here. Children don't seem to make the transition from children's club to youth group well. They disappear out into the big, wide world at this point, never to be seen again – I'm overdramatising, but you will get the point. There are several things we can do to stop this happening:

Overlap of Ages – Children can stay part of the children's club until they are twelve, but can join the youth programme when they are eleven. This allows them still to be the "big person" in children's club while they are finding their feet in the youth group.

Overlap of Leaders – Some of the leaders who work in the children's club also work in the youth club. Familiar faces are very comforting when you've joined a strange new world.

Buddy System – For the first six months the new addition is looked after by a named teenager who makes sure all is well and helps them adjust to the new environment.

The youth and children's departments must work incredibly closely – we have heard much of joined-up government, and this is about joined-up church. Not independent departments but interdependent teams.

If you have managed to bring a new child into a children's small group, then allow them to move into a youth small group. They are already used to the small-group environment and can simply move to a youth discipleship group, where they can continue their journey to spiritual maturity. It is also a good idea to move the children in groups rather than as individuals, so they move on with their friends.

FIRST CONTACT
(Schools' Ministry)

My daughter recently started school. It was an emotional morning. She was very excited; my wife and I were very nervous. She put on her little school uniform. She collected her packed lunch with the obligatory "Barbie" logo. She put on her newly polished shoes and took her mother's hand for the short journey to school. She loved it. She talked about it all evening. Then, just after her bedtime story, she looked serious and said:

"Daddy, do I have to go to school for a long time?"

She was only four. I didn't have the heart to tell her that she could be in the education system for the next 18 years. But this is the reality. Thousands and thousands of children every day make their way to school. If we want to talk to children, then that's where they are.

As well as the large number of church schools, there exists at present an opening for Christians to have input into a huge number of non-church schools. Not just as governors or as part of the large body of excellent Christian teachers, but as Christian workers who come in for the purpose of taking Christian assemblies or Religious Education classes.

Being able to work in schools is a major opportunity. Being able to take school assemblies means that you can stand in front of hundreds of children, who are supervised by school teachers, and within certain limits share the principles of God's word. If you are good at what you do and the school staff warm to you then you could be invited in with an ever-increasing frequency. The law requires that schools provide Christian assemblies, but teachers for the most part don't like taking assemblies (when I talked to a teacher about this she mentioned that standing in front of the children is not the thing that puts them off; it is the number of other teachers watching. Clearly teachers who are not Christians themselves sometimes find it difficult to present Christian assemblies). Schools will be very keen to have your input, but herein lies the problem. You could get to the point where the school would like you to come in several times a week. A huge percentage of your time could be spent in schools. Before this happens it is important to know why you are there.

Over recent years schools' ministry has gained an increasingly high profile, and a very large number of churches now have input into local schools. However, it is not legitimate to have input into schools just because everyone else is doing it! There are two legitimate reasons for being involved in schools' ministry:

1. To be salt and light

The Bible is clear that the Kingdom of God is within us. When a Christian enters a school, the Kingdom of God comes to the school. Simply because a Christian is there the light begins to shine. Before we say a word, the light begins to shine. Going into schools to bring salt and light is a worthwhile investment. Hundreds of children will be able to see and hear Jesus in you. *We may be the only Christians some of these children ever see and we should never undervalue our role or our responsibility.*

2. As a means of drawing children into your children's club

Children who see you in school assembly may want to come to your children's club because you've personally invited them. Parents may be more inclined to allow their children to come to your children's club because they know that you are allowed into their school.

WARNING

Because of the above I recommend that you do not advertise your children's club in a school unless you have had input into that school for at least six months. It will take you six months to build a relationship with the school and the head teacher. Relationship is everything. With the best will in the world, sometimes things go wrong at children's clubs. A broken bone on a bouncy castle, a child who runs off early and takes hours to be found, a fight... The list is endless. If something goes wrong in your club and you have only been in the school for a few weeks, the negative effect may cause problems in the club and the school may close the door to you. If, however, you have a working relationship, then most head teachers will allow you to explain the difficulty and, since most experienced heads have encountered every difficulty known to man (with the possible exception of plague and famine), they will understand that sometimes things go wrong.

Many churches have built strong and well-attended children's clubs by focusing on schools' ministry. Even children's workers who are not full-time may be able to find the several hours a week (or possibly a month) that it takes to give input into the school. I have recently come across a project called "Open the Book". A small team goes into a school once a week to read a story from *The Lion Bible for Children*. It can be a very simple reading, or the group can act bits out or use props they have made or get the children involved – all dependent on the ability and skills of the team. They then go to someone's house nearby for a coffee and to sort out the following week. There is no searching for ideas, no pressure, and it is being undertaken by young mums and retired people, who may have not got involved otherwise.

The best scenario is a combination of (1) and (2). Be salt and light, but also use the opportunity to populate your children's programmes.

So you've worked out why you want to have input, but now how do you get into the school?

The importance of prayer should never be overlooked. Your presence in school is of vital significance. Light is about to enter the place and any lurking darkness will not be too pleased. So before you attempt to make contact, pray. Make it a theme for your prayer meetings; ask people to make it part of their daily devotions.

COMMENT

It is unfortunate that over the many years I have been involved in schools I have always had less of a problem gaining access and consistently inputting into the school when the head teacher has been an agnostic or an atheist than when the head teacher has been of a religious persuasion. I have always done my utmost not to fly denominational colours when entering a school, but when the head teacher is a Baptist he wants Baptist input. When the head teacher is from a Pentecostal background she wants Pentecostal input. This is complete nonsense. We need as much CHRISTIAN input into a school as possible, and fighting our party's position is at best very counter-productive.

Once you have prayed and made the whole thing a matter of ongoing prayer it is useful to enquire whether there is a Christian teacher in the school who might invite you in, or recommend you to the person who does the inviting. If there is nobody in the school who can recommend you, then phone the school and ask for ten minutes with the head teacher to discuss your request.

After the above we move into the area of cold-calling. You could send a letter advising the teacher of what you can do. You can phone the school and try to book a one-off assembly. These are much more difficult routes, but don't be put off – they can work.

It is certainly true that the first school you make contact with is the hardest. I have now taken well over 3,000 school assemblies! I don't have a problem with them any more. If I have to change areas or want to make contact with new schools then I ask the old schools for a reference. I then give a copy to the new school. If you work in a city, you will know as I do how quickly teachers move around. Teachers who liked your assemblies may become head teachers and they will want you in their new school. Collect references – they show that you are credible. Back to the original point. The first school is always the hardest. Stick with it.

● First Contact

When you are scheduled to be in school you should always dress smartly and never wear blue jeans – even if the teachers do. Be professional, be courteous and helpful, particularly to the secretary you meet at reception – a primary-school secretary carries a lot more responsibility and influence than we would ever warrant. Arrive on time, calm and relaxed – this will put all those around you into a similar frame of mind. Now balance all that with the fact that you are the ambassador of the King of all kings and life comes to every place where you step. It's a tricky balance – to walk with boldness and humility.

● Conducting the Assembly or Lesson

You may be asked how you want to be introduced. I always opt for the simplest response:

"Tell them my name is Mark, and I've come to talk to them."

No denominational ties, no titles, no frills, just me. This generation doesn't understand denominations and this generation has very little respect for authority. In fact, children are taught from the earliest age to distrust it. One head teacher introduced me as follows:

"This is Rev. Mark Griffiths, and he has come to tell us what Christians believe."

From the moment I walked to the front the children were wearing their "impress us if you can vicar" faces. The head teacher had successfully built massive barriers between them and me, barriers which I would have to spend precious assembly time pulling down before I could communicate anything. I went for the direct approach and hoped that I could smooth it over with the headmaster later. I said:

"Hi, you can call me Mark and I'm here to tell you what anyone with a brain believes!"

I got away with it. The headmaster smiled and we got on great from that point. The children's demeanour changed and they were very responsive.

Be fun, be entertaining, but don't be the clown. Conduct the assembly with the same standards of discipline as the head teacher would. When you stand at the front then you are in charge. Don't be afraid to ask a child who is misbehaving to stop.

● What Do You Talk About?

Here are some pointers:

❑ Be relevant, talk about bullies, heroes, worries, caring, and divorce
❑ Use stories, drama, object lessons, and involvement
❑ Don't just give the children information, teach them how to learn

But for expert help on what to say, I suggest the following:

❑ *77 Talks for 21st Century Kids* by Chris Chesterton
❑ *52 Ideas for Junior Classroom Assemblies* by Chris Chesterton and Pat Gutteridge
❑ *77 Talks for Cyberspace Kids* by Chris Chesterton and David T. Ward
❑ *52 Ideas for Infant School Assemblies* by Chris Chesterton and Elaine Buckley
❑ *Fusion* by Mark Griffiths (use the stories only)
❑ *Impact* by Mark Griffiths (use the stories only)

All published by Monarch Books

● Staying In

So you are in. How do you stay in? As in most areas of Christian ministry, relationship is the key. It may seem like a waste of time to sit in a staff room drinking coffee, but this is the place where the teachers are making decisions on whether they would like you back or not. Be friendly, be approachable, be fun. Here are some basics:

❑ Learn the head teacher's name
❑ Show authentic interest in the school
❑ Always send Christmas cards
❑ Be human!
❑ Never carry gossip about one school to another
❑ Never let the school down unless you are dying or dead!

● Administration – Making Life Simpler

I send out a letter in every term (a sample is shown in the Appendix). In early September I will send out a letter advertising the assemblies available for September, October, November and December. The schools will then phone or e-mail and book an assembly date for September, October, November and December. By mid-September all my administration regarding schools is complete and I can concentrate on taking assemblies. It really is quite liberating. I then send out a letter in December for January, February and March and a final letter in April for June and July. I don't take assemblies in April because of the huge amount of school holiday then and I don't take assemblies in May because that's my month for refocusing.

Once I have developed an assembly and used it for the whole month I write it up properly and place it in a file with all the necessary visuals. I now have 45 key assemblies that I rotate in a five-year cycle.

I also tend to offer assemblies in threes, following this pattern:

Month 1: Moral teaching that may have a limited Christian content
Month 2: Much stronger Christian content
Month 3: Strong Christian content (Christmas and Easter usually fall in my third month)

(I add an extra assembly in the Christmas term because I use the opportunity in September's assembly to mention the relaunch of the children's club usually in the last couple of weeks of September or first week of October).

WARNING

It is possible to be too popular! I quickly arrived at the point where most of the 66 primary schools within the city welcomed my input. It is tempting to visit them all. But can we really work our purposes out in every school? It is best to mark yourself a geographical limit – I will visit schools within five kilometres of the church, or I will only visit schools within my parish boundary. I may visit other schools but only for specials: harvest festivals, Christmas, Easter, OFSTED inspections. In reality I have always found it very hard to say no and still sometimes travel 8 or 9km to take an assembly – you don't have to follow my bad habits!

MISCONCEPTIONS

If I were to wear spectacles with rose-coloured lenses the world would look pink; if I wore blue lenses the world would look far colder. We all wear spectacles over our minds. These spectacles are called preconceptions. We all have them. They colour the way we see things, and are placed there as a result of our upbringing, our first experiences with church, our denomination and our social class.

When I first became a Christian I was put in charge of a Sunday school class and really didn't know what I was doing. After spending several weeks learning pop songs with the ten- and eleven-year-olds that I was responsible for, I was eventually given a "pack" of stuff from a reputable Christian supplier which contained charts and game ideas and the like. It soon became very clear to me that the group enjoyed the pop songs much more. But this "pack" was what I was supposed to teach, and teach it I did, no matter how depressed everyone else in the group looked – I cringe when I think back on it now. The only representation of Christ this group was getting was dull, uninspiring and lifeless. I kept this up for many months despite the fact that the group of ten became a group of five. Someone told me that they always drop out when they get a bit older!

Eventually the group was reprieved and I went off to theological college for three years to learn how to do it properly. The very scary part was that the college reinforced the model I was already using – I occasionally lecture on children's ministry at the same college now, so hopefully the model is slowly being eroded. Three years later I returned for a short period to the church that I had left, and in that time, with my new enthusiasm, I became the Sunday school superintendent. (I'm still not quite sure what one of them is: I couldn't find this particular ministry gift in my Bible.)

Now this is where the preconception comes in. When it became time for me to start teaching I did what I had seen. I placed one person in charge of lots of little groups split by age and gave each leader a "pack" and told them to get on with it. It was nonsense. I knew it didn't work; I knew the children didn't respond; I knew it wasn't what God was looking for, but this was what I knew – this was my preconception of children's ministry and my preconception was undoubtedly a *mis*conception. It just didn't work.

Eventually I had to get on my knees before God and allow him to strip the preconceptions away. Now I am always challenging what we do, always challenging the preconception, always asking:

Why do we do it this way?
and Is this really working?

It keeps me fresh, but it's never easy to remove the preconceptions, especially if we've been running our programme based on them for a long time.

It is probably worthwhile spending a little time here looking at some other misconceptions that may affect what we are building.

Change the Format Every Week

This is a common misconception. It is probably best explained by a short story:

Little Jim turns up at the children's club for the first time. His mum ruffles his hair, kisses him on the cheek and tells him to have a good time and she will be back for him later. He walks into the club discreetly wiping the kiss off his cheek. He hands in his registration form and walks into the hall. The chairs are facing the front. He chooses a seat that is empty and sits down. The songs are first and so he watches the others, and then after a couple of songs he tries to join in. He doesn't know the words, but he's going to have a try. He watches the games, he listens to the announcements and then he sits through the talk time. He's enjoyed it, but he hasn't actually learned anything because insecure people don't learn. And on his first visit he is certainly insecure. At the end of the evening he leaves. His mum is waiting. She asks him how it went; he tells her it was good. She asks if he is coming again; he says yes. They go home.

The following week he's back. He's not new now so he announces his name, gets it ticked off the register and boldly enters the club. Then to his horror he discovers the seats are now facing in the opposite direction. He's insecure again. He's not going to learn tonight – he's insecure again, and insecure people don't learn. He listens to the songs and eventually joins in; he watches the games, he hears the talk, he leaves. Mum asks him how it went; he says it was OK. She asks him if he's coming again and he says, probably. They go home.

One week later Jim is back. He walks in to discover the seats are now all gone. It's praise party night. He doesn't know what to do, where to go, where to sit. He's insecure again. He's not going to learn tonight. In fact when mum asks him the question at the end of the night his answer is no. He's not coming back again.

Little Jim lives with mum; his sister lives with dad at the other end of town with his stepbrothers. Dad left last year, and he's an insecure little boy. He's not unusual. Our "Change the Format Every Week" motif keeps insecure children insecure.

For some reason that I have not been able to work out, we are preoccupied now with shaking people out of their comfort zones. I hear it preached a lot. But I am not sure why I need to leave my comfort zone. I like being secure; the Bible tells me that being under the shadow of God's wing is a good place to be – in a comfort zone. Things don't always go well for me. Sometimes I have to walk through some difficult situations and I do so from my position of being under the shadow of God's wing. You see, we don't have to leave the security of God to go off and fight our battle: he comes with us. We fight from a position of security. Secure people change things.

Let's allow our children to arrive to a warm welcome. Let's make it clear what they can and can't do. Let's keep the format consistent. Let's build secure children.

Everyone Does Everything

I've seen this one on the wall of some children's clubs under the heading RULES. Let me expose this one quickly. We stand at the front and tell the children that they are all unique, special and different and behind them under the word RULES is this misconception.

It follows the pattern that when there is a game being played, everyone plays the game. Many will protest and squeal:

"We don't like playing games!"

Our response comes: "In here everyone does everything; it's a rule."

You become known as the club that plays games, so all the children that like playing games come to your club. All the children that hate games don't. They go to the local Baptist church where they can do crafts, because they like crafts; or to the Anglican church where they play computer games, or to the Pentecostals, who have a good tuck shop. We have successfully reintroduced denominations.

God gave us free will enshrined in the glorious word CHOICE. Why do they have to go elsewhere to do the things they like? Why can't the children who like games come in and play games, and the children who like crafts come in and do crafts, and those who like computer games come in and do that? And after playing computer games for a while why can't they then go and make something in crafts? And then, after having all those options for an hour, why can't they sit down for teaching and praise? I can't think of any reason.

If we really believe that they are special and unique and different, then let's allow them to *be* special and unique and different, and give them choices.

Why do we do it this way? Is this really working? You will have to look at your group honestly and answer these questions for yourself.

And a new question – Is what we do consistent with what we teach? Let's not fall into the trap of telling the children one thing in our preaching and then having something completely contradictory in our RULES.

There are more misconceptions that come to mind, but they are embedded in the legacy of a man named Robert Raikes.

ROBERT RAIKES' LEGACY

The character of many of the youngsters was transformed. Their swearing, rudeness, and unruliness was replaced by a sense of duty.

It could be a quote from a strong advocate for National Service. It's not. The quote is over 300 years old and isn't describing a new police initiative or government reform, it is something more radical than that. The transformation in question was the result of Sunday school attendance. Sunday school is the great-great-grandparent of the Christian children's club.

Sunday schools stretch way back in history. The first recorded Sunday schools were started in 1756 in Gloucester by a newspaper owner named Robert Raikes. The first Sunday saw over 100 children attend and less than a decade later most cities, towns and villages had their own Sunday school.

In this day of rising crime, particularly among the young, I should add that there was another interesting by-product of Sunday school: the crime rate dropped sharply in Raikes' city and county. At the Easter Quarter Sessions of 1786, the magistrates passed a unanimous vote of thanks for the benefits of Sunday schools to the morals of the young. Maybe someone should tell the Home Secretary.

There is no doubt that Robert Raikes was a godly man who heard from God. But there are some negative aspects to the Sunday school legacy:

- The place of teaching moved from the home to a building
- The time for teaching moved from "day-to-day" to Sunday
- The teacher was no longer the parent but the professional Sunday school teacher

The first two points were discussed in an earlier chapter, but it would seem that the most enduring outcome of Raikes' legacy has been the position of the Sunday school teacher.

As we discussed in the previous chapter under misconceptions, sometimes we embrace things because of our own background and upbringing that may not necessarily be right for today. Whilst there are still a huge number of Sunday schools and mid-week clubs that keep to Robert Raikes' pattern, it must be stated that this is not a biblical pattern. The pattern is only 300 years old, but it has become so ingrained into popular church culture that one would think that it came as a direct statement from Jesus himself. This is the pattern:

There is one teacher (or, where good child-protection policies are in place, a teacher and a helper) and they have a class which is theirs. They teach this class week in, week out. The fortunate ones have a teenage helper. Their class is all of the same age and often the same sex. So one teacher will be in charge of the ten-year-old girls, another teacher will be in charge of the seven-year-old boys, etc. Let me state again that this pattern is not from the Bible: it is from Robert Raikes. It is loaded with potential difficulties. It means that the teacher had better contain the full counsel of God. She had better contain all the gifts of God wrapped up in one body. In short she had better be a super-apostle. The reason? She is all the ten-year-old girls will ever get this year, so she has to be everything.

The problem with this pattern is that it flies in the face of what I believe God has been trying to do towards the end of the last millennium.

Again, there are a lot of factors to balance here. God is committed to the priesthood of all believers. Since Calvary we all have the right to boldly approach the throne of God. We are all priests. Church leadership has tried to make the difficult transition from one man doing everything to a team of people ministering, involving lay ministry. This model better reflects the priesthood of all believers. But there is a missing factor. Yes, God wants us all to approach him with boldness; yes we are all ministers, but from the dawn of time until the end of time God still raises up men and women who are in themselves gifts to the church, people whom God has called to be apostles, evangelists, prophets, pastors and teachers, as mentioned in Ephesians 4. These gifts are important, because the Bible tells us they exist:

> *so that his people would learn to serve and his body would grow strong.*
> (Ephesians 4:12)

I am a firm believer in God-given directional leadership. ***Strong leadership is a prerequisite of a strong church. Weak, compromising leadership leads to weak, compromised churches. But understand: strong does not mean proud or arrogant; in fact the opposite is true.***

There is a whole range of gifted people that God wants to release into our children's ministry, but while we insist on sitting one teacher on the seat with her group then we hinder this. There are people with a pastoral gift who would love to get alongside the children who are hurting or wounded or in need of help in your group, but they can't because the only people you allow in are those who will teach their small group. We complain endlessly that we never have enough people, but we restrict people's ability to help.

The difficulty is, to make this happen we can no longer have classes split according to age and gender. We need to bring them together as a larger group. This causes some people a huge problem:

"How can a five-year-old and an eleven-year-old learn in the same class?"

It is a fair question. And if we were teaching mathematics or English literature or geography, it is very unlikely that the five-year-old and the eleven-year-old could learn together. However, I don't teach mathematics or English literature, I proclaim the gospel; the timeless gospel that Jesus proclaimed; the gospel that young and old came to listen to together; the one where grannies and grandchildren sat side by side to hear and each understand on their own level; *the timeless gospel, which sometimes bypasses the brain and hits the heart;* the glorious gospel, which transforms young and old, which confuses the Pharisee but leaves the young boy saying:

"I have these fish and loaves; will they help?"

It is also worth pointing out that we should always have a long-term view of children's ministry. The five-year-old may not "get it" today, but we are expecting to present the same lesson to them in four years' time. If we combine our groups then we allow the whole range of God-given gifts to function. Here are some examples of the gifts that can be released into children's ministry if we change the paradigm:

Pastors: Obviously the word most closely associated with this would be shepherding – to care for the flock. When Jesus talks to Peter at the end of John's Gospel he extols him to "take care of my sheep". This is what we are looking for within this gift – someone who can take care of God's lambs; someone with an affinity for getting alongside those who are hurting or needy or simply those who need to feel loved. We are all called to pastor, but there are people who excel in this area. They may not be the best teachers or leaders, and their administration skills may be non-existent, but their ability to care sets them apart as people we desperately need within the context of children's ministry.

Administrators: Not just those who can count the money from the tuck shop, but those with a clear, God-given ability to organise: to ensure that everything is set up on time, that the registers are correct, and the rent is paid. As you will see in the chapter on infrastructure, these people are as important to the growth and development of your work as are the evangelists.

Evangelists: Which leads us nicely to the evangelists: those with an ability to make the gospel bite-sized and easily digestible, those with an ability to reap the harvest and to inspire and equip others to do the same. Part of my gifting lies here: I can fill buildings with children by accident when others spend months on achieving the same thing by design. It's an area of gifting, but a caution is necessary: evangelists can fill your club, but if you have only evangelists they will also empty it again. They may refill it shortly afterwards, but it will be with a completely different group. They need to be surrounded by lots of other gifting.

Hospitality: When our project used to run on a Saturday the leaders would arrive a couple of hours early and eat breakfast together and pray together before the club began. It was not my idea. Someone with the gift of hospitality said they would like to do it for us – nobody objected. People with this gift facilitate the building of teams. They may never want to be directly involved with teaching the children, but that doesn't mean they can't use their gift within the children's clubs or to welcome the children as they arrive.

Apostles: Don't get put off by this word. Apostle is simply another gift. It is not more special than the others. Apostles are those with an affinity for making Jesus known in places where Jesus is not known. They have an ability to build. They can be incredibly visionary and see what needs to happen to fulfil the vision. They can develop new projects, they can proclaim the gospel, they can administer, but they still need the support of others.

We pray for the workers with the right gifts – for teachers and pastors, for administrators with gifts of administration and those with wisdom, for those with faith and those with the gift of help and service. We pray that we'll use each person in the area of their gifting, for them to grow and feel fulfilled by the role they play and as a role model for the children.

A NEW GENERATION OF LEADERS

John Blanchard was a lieutenant in the Second World War. His hobby was reading books. I know this may not seem like the sort of thing lieutenants in the US Navy would do, but whenever he had free time John would sneak off to the library. On this particular day he had gone to the library and picked up a book bound in light-blue material from the shelf. He began to read but was distracted by the comments that had been written in the margins of the book by someone whom he guessed was the book's previous owner.

Sure enough, at the end of the book was the name and address of the previous owner: one Hollis Maynell, who lived in New York City. He wrote to her and simply said that he enjoyed her comments. She wrote back. One year and one month of writing then took place and the two formed a loving relationship within these letters. But, no matter how many times John asked, Hollis refused to send him a photograph.

Eventually they arranged to meet. The time set was 7pm. The place, Grand Central Station. She would wear a rose and he would be identified by the blue-bound book in which he had first read her comments.

He arrived at the station in his best dress uniform and saw a lady walking towards him. I will let him describe the scene from here:

A young woman was coming toward me; her figure was long and slim. Her blonde hair lay back in curls from her delicate ears; her eyes as blue as flowers. Her lips and chin had a gentle firmness, and in her pale green suit she was like springtime come alive. I started toward her entirely forgetting to notice that she was not wearing a rose. As I moved, a small provocative smile curved her lips. "Going my way, sailor?" she murmured.

Almost uncontrollably I made one step closer to her, and then I saw Hollis Maynell.

She was standing almost directly behind the girl. A woman well past 40, she had greying hair tucked under a hat. She was more than plump, her thick-ankled feet thrust into low-heeled shoes. The girl in the pale green suit was quickly walking away. I thought I was split in two, so keen was my desire to follow her, and yet so deep was my longing for the woman whose spirit had truly companioned me and upheld my own.

And there she stood. Her pale, plump face was gentle and sensible; her grey eyes had a warm and kindly twinkle. I did not hesitate. I squared my shoulders and saluted:

"I am Lt John Blanchard. I am so glad you could meet me. May I take you to dinner?"

The woman's face broadened into a tolerant smile...

There is more to this story, but let's look at this subject of developing leaders a little first. ***It is certain that your ability to reproduce leaders will be THE SINGLE MOST IMPORTANT factor that will determine the extent of your vision.*** When children's workers have been asked to write down what topics they would like covered in seminars, this one always comes up: "How do I get more leaders?" In many ways it is not about how well we run the race; it is about how many people we get running. So how do we do it? How do we develop leaders?

Be a Leader – There has been much talk in recent years about the role of leaders in the church context. I believe in the plurality of leadership; I am also a huge supporter of the whole congregation rising up and fulfilling their role in the body of Christ. But I am also a passionate believer in God-given leadership. From the dawn of time until the end of time God insists on raising up individuals who will bring clear direction to his people. Be that kind of leader. ***Lead with compassion, conviction and courage, and people will follow you.*** Lead by democratic committee and change your views according to popular consent, and you are going nowhere.

We must start with a vision – Proverbs 29:18 tells us:

Where there is no vision, the people perish.

The applications for this verse are numerous. Clearly, in its context, it is talking about a vision of God. But the principle can allow a wider interpretation. If people have nothing to aim for, nothing to run after, nothing that consumes and motivates them, then they will:

● dwell carelessly (NIV)
● cast off restraint (NKJ)
● run wild (NLT)
● perish (KJV)

People need something to pursue. Sir Ernest Shackleton, the famous explorer, placed an advertisement in a newspaper in 1900:

Men wanted for hazardous adventure. Small wages, long months of complete darkness, constant danger, and safe return doubtful. Honour and recognition in case of success.

He commented that it seemed as though half of England had responded to the advert. People wanted something to run after. Visionary people often attract a following. People will come with you if they know that you are going somewhere. We recruit to a vision, and never simply ask for volunteers. When Jesus approached the disciples, he said:

Follow me and I will make you fishers of men. (Matthew 4:19)

He was recruiting to a vision.

Write the vision down – Habakkuk 2:2 says:

Then the Lord told me: "I will give you my message in the form of a vision. Write it clearly enough to be read at a glance."

It is often not until the vision is actually written down that it can begin to be outworked. Writing it down means that the visionary mind has to put into words what it has seen and felt and perceived. This is a very important part of the process. It needs to be easily understood and, as God's instruction to Habakkuk points out, it needs to be clear. This is particularly important, because the next stage is to share it with others.

Start with a small group – Jesus' message would change the world. But to get that message around the world he started with a small group and poured his life into them. Often they missed it; often they completely misunderstood what the prime directive was, but he continued to pour himself into this group. We need to learn from this. If we can share the vision with six to twelve people and do so in such a way that they begin to claim the vision as their own, then they in turn will gather people around themselves and so the vision begins to spread. And then we are up and running. We have an inner core of leaders who will share the message with the next level of leaders, and so on.

Keep recruiting – I Samuel 14:52 gives us an insight into King Saul at his best, when it says:

So whenever King Saul saw a young man who was brave and strong, he drafted him into his army. (NLT)

King Saul's philosophy was simple – constant recruitment. When I spend my summers taking children's camps, or when I travel around the country taking leadership development sessions, I am not averse to seeing a person who clearly has the hand of God on their life and inviting them to come and work with me. It is the King Saul philosophy. The philosophy has another attribute.

It means we don't make the mistake of trying to fill positions. *King Saul was not about filling positions; he was about bringing people of character on board.* These sorts of people will create their own position; just get them on board.

The leaders you have or seek to bring on board will fall into four categories:

+ Leaders who add to what you are doing. Keep them, they are a blessing, but work with them, they may be able to do more than that.

− Leaders who subtract from what you are doing: those who drop the drinks tray in the middle of your appeal; those who can't seem to make it to meetings on time. Work with these. Ultimately they may have to step down, but not before we have invested enough time and energy and prayer in them to be able to say we did our best.

X Leaders who multiply what you do: those for whom everything they touch turns to gold; those who can take on the failing project and make it happen. These people are like gold. Never take them for granted.

÷ Leaders who are divisive; leaders who undermine. This one is very simple. You ask them to leave as quickly as possible. Don't entertain them. Don't allow them to compromise what God is doing. This may seem cold, but it is so important.

Get your leaders recruiting – Once your leaders have captured your heart then allow them to recruit as well. Allow them to form their own teams under them. They are all still working out the vision that you presented to them, but now they own it. Don't get upset if it looks a little different from what you intended. Keep your eye on the end result. If you are still on course for the end goal then be secure enough to allow your leaders some room for interpretation of the vision as they begin to mature and develop.

Set standards for your workers – There are some basics that must be present in their lives. Remember, these leaders will be the examples that the children look to in order to model their lives. They must have a genuine relationship with God, read their Bibles and pray regularly, live lives that reflect Christian values, have a sense of fun and life, and show a willingness to be teachable. In all this there are still important issues regarding whom we recruit as leaders. I have been horrified by the number of stories I have heard recently of paedophiles targeting churches. The Criminal Records Bureau now allows us to police-check everyone who works with children. If they can fulfil their promise of clearing 80% of applications in three weeks then there is no need to place a person in position until the police check has cleared. I never allow a person to be alone with a child or group of children. My groups are always taught by at least two people. We can no longer blindly trust people, so be very diligent in this area. Incorporating teenagers into this area (which I am always keen to do) still requires that two adults be present.

Your leaders are like gold – Without them the impact of the vision will be greatly diminished. Love them sincerely and show genuine appreciation and pray for them regularly. Ensure that they have opportunities for training.

> ## TIP
>
> **Meet regularly and also remember to meet socially. Have fun with them. The motto must be WORK HARD and PLAY HARD. Bowl together, ski together, walk together, laugh together – even cry together!**

And now I will give you the key to leadership development. The key to ensuring that you always have a strong leadership base for many years to come. Are you ready? OK, here it is:

Recruit your leaders when they reach the age of twelve!

I know this is loaded with difficulty; I know most of them have no concept of responsibility; I know that most of them fall in the "–" leadership category. They are hard work. But if you can carry them through the first couple of years, by age fourteen you begin to see what incredible leaders you are producing. By age sixteen you have leaders of excellence. And they never ever turn around and say:

"We've never done it this way before."

They know how you think, and how you work. They came through your children's programmes, they know what you do, and they are living proof that it works. They will still mess up. They will still be easily distracted and turn up late for your meetings because the boy/girl down the street needed to talk to them, but they are worth the investment. You must out of necessity restrict the areas your young leaders are involved in: for example they may do visitation with you, but never on their own. It may be worthwhile having a monthly discipleship/training meeting just for your younger leaders; it is worth talking this through with your youth department first and ensuring that you are not overloading their schedule (remember the link between youth and children's workers is always very important).

And now back to Lieutenant John Blanchard.

> *"I am Lt John Blanchard. I am so glad you could meet me. May I take you to dinner?"*
>
> *The woman's face broadened into a tolerant smile.*
>
> *"I don't know what this is about, son," she answered "But that young lady in the green suit who just went by, she begged me to wear this rose on my coat. And she said if you asked me to dinner, I should tell you she is waiting in the big restaurant across the street. She said it was some kind of test."*

Hollis Maynell knew that she wanted to be with someone who was prepared to look deeper than a pretty face. This was about more than appearance; this was about the heart.

And therein lies the basis of this chapter. We may not find the most qualified leaders, we may never find the most gifted leaders, but if we can find people who love children and whose hearts are right then we will never go far wrong. Skills and procedures we can teach; the right heart-spirit is something the person must arrive with.

Don't try and build with people who look good, build with people who have the right heart. They may not have a burden for children's work, but they can get that from you. They might not understand the practical implications, but they can get that from you as well. But a teachable spirit and a right heart are foundation stones.

God spends his time looking for a builder whose heart is right. God is not worried about what will be built, for if the heart of the builder is right then the building will be just fine. God is looking for "wise master builders" and that title is given to people whose hearts are right.

VISION NEEDS PROVISION

Is it possible to run a children's ministry that is self-sufficient? Or will children's ministry always need to be supported by the local church? Can the children's club stand alone in terms of personnel and finances?

This is a major issue. If we are truly serious about being able to church-plant from the children's club upwards then it is clear that we need to be able to establish a strong financial base. When I began work in my last church I placed a statement of intent on the wall. It read:

I aim to:
1. *Make the gospel of Jesus Christ known to as many children as possible, as fast as possible, using the best possible methods, and give these children an opportunity to respond to the gospel*
2. *Equip others to do the same*
3. *Develop child-based businesses that will finance the above*

I was determined to prove, before I moved to another church, that a children's department could be self-financing. Ten years later we had £25,000 in our children's department account, employed two full-time staff and 22 part-time staff in our children's activities, and our turnover in the last financial year was £150,000. My own salary also came from this account. Let me make sure that this is clear: this was the children's department, not the main church.

I will outline how this was accomplished, but I must preface it with the usual warning. What worked for us may not work for you. It is principles that I am trying to communicate and not necessarily practice.

The first business opportunity that presented itself was to run an after-school project in our church. Several parents had contacted us to ask if we provided such a service, so eventually, after giving the matter some consideration, we went ahead and launched it. We ran from September to December with three children and a staff of two volunteers. It did not look good, but we decided to keep going. We needed to borrow £4,500 from the main church to buy a minibus and added a little more to the debt with publicity – this involved me in forfeiting one month's salary to offset the amount if I didn't repay the loan within twelve months! We contacted the schools that were close by – I already had a relationship with them because of our successful assembly programme – and asked them to distribute our publicity.

Our numbers began to increase dramatically. We offered the first week free and our numbers increased even further. We now had fifteen children paying £15 a week each in a hall we owned, staffed by two volunteers. We paid for the minibus within six months. The local Chamber of Commerce then decided to give us some money to help us expand. And so the momentum had begun.

We then realised that our after-school club would not provide for the children during holidays, so we added a play scheme. We then realised that this could be repeated in other parts of the city. We also added in a breakfast club for children whose parents start work before school begins.

Maybe some definitions will help at this point:

After-school Projects

After-school projects are the fastest-growing form of out-of-school childcare. Some are based in schools, some in community halls and some in other venues. The children are usually collected from their school by a member of the childcare team and taken to the venue – walked or transported by minibus depending on the location of the venue. A wide range of activities will then be available to the children, including pool, table tennis, crafts, construction, sports, imaginary play, computer games, etc. A snack is provided, which some of the children have the opportunity to help prepare. The children stay at the project until their parents collect them. Duration of stay at the project varies from 30 minutes to three hours (the projects close at 6pm). But stimulating and wholesome activities are encouraged so that no matter how long the stay, it is enjoyable and full of fun.

Holiday Play Schemes

Most out-of-school-hours childcare is used by working parents. Holiday play schemes seem be the exception. A large number of attendees at holiday play schemes are children just looking for an exciting alternative to sitting at home during the school holidays. Most projects provide a wider range of activities for their holiday play schemes than they do for their other projects. Many also offer outside activities such as roller-skating, ice-skating and day trips for the children who attend. Unlike after-school and breakfast clubs there is usually no drop off/pick up service available. Parents bring their children to the venue in the morning and collect them at the end of the day. We spend an hour of each holiday play scheme day presenting a Bible-based teaching programme – similar to that in the *Fusion* and *Impact* curriculum series.

Breakfast Clubs

Breakfast clubs are a relatively new concept, but are an incredibly important addition to out-of-school childcare. Many parents have to start work earlier than their children start school. Because of this, many complicated and elaborate arrangements have to be made with neighbours and relatives. In some new towns this network of neighbours and relatives just does not exist. Breakfast clubs run in a variety of locations. They usually start quite early to enable parents to drop off their children at the childcare facility on their way to work. The breakfast club then provides activities and breakfast. If the club is based at the child's school, they simply leave the club at the appropriate time and go to their classroom. Where the club isn't based at the school, the children are walked or taken by minibus to their school in time for school to start.

Apart from the holiday play scheme, where we have the opportunity to present a Bible-based curriculum, the other projects have very little Christian input other than giving thanks in prayer before they eat their snack. The childcare-based projects achieve the following:

- They meet a clearly identifiable community need
- They raise the profile of the local church
- They provide an excellent opportunity to invite children to your outreach club
- THEY FINANCE THE PRESENTATION OF THE GOSPEL

It is vitally important to realise why the above exist. If we fall into the trap of thinking they are ways of presenting the gospel then we make a mistake: they finance the proclamation of the gospel. There is a huge difference.

At the point when I handed in my notice at Christian Centre and began the move to St Mary's, Bletchley, we had eight after-school projects, four

---

WARNING

I suspect God didn't call you to run a business. I hope that God called you to win boys and girls to Jesus, to extend the Kingdom, to proclaim the gospel. Running a business takes time and energy. As soon as is financially possible you MUST hire a business manager, someone who can effectively take care of the day-to-day running of the business, freeing you up to do what God called you to do. It still means you have to make the directional decisions, and from time to time there will be difficulties that only you can solve. But the day-to-day responsibility does not lie with you.

holiday play schemes and a breakfast club. We fulfilled the aim very well. They are the child-based businesses that finance ministry, meet community needs and give the church profile.

There is one closing comment I would like to make. In my next church placement, I would not seek to place after-school projects all over the city; I would aim for one centralised project that could cater for larger numbers. I would seek to do the same with the play scheme and also with the breakfast club. This would allow the outreach club, the after-school project, the play scheme and the breakfast club to operate out of the same building.

VISITATION, RECORD–KEEPING AND INFRASTRUCTURE

It would be easy to underestimate the significance of this chapter for our children's club. But I would suggest that the items in this chapter contribute significantly to producing and sustaining large children's clubs – I would go as far as to say that if your club has no visitation programme, no record-keeping and no infrastructure it will seriously struggle to maintain large attendance for any period of time.

Possibly the best way to explain the procedures and practices that underpin a children's club is to describe the process from first attendance. When a child first attends the children's club they must come with a parent or guardian, or attend with a completed registration form. The registration form should contain at least the information shown opposite.

There are implications under the Data Protection Act here, and you should contact the address given in the Appendix for further information before you start storing names and addresses either manually or on computer.

There are other items that can be added, such as doctor's name, surgery address, etc.

Once the information has been given it should be

REGISTRATION FORM

This form must be completed before your child attends one of our activities

Child's Name: _____

Address: _____

_____

_____

Telephone Number: _____ DoB: _____

Secondary Contact Number: _____

School Attended: _____

Medical conditions we should be aware of: _____

_____

_____

In case of major accident, your child will be taken, by ambulance if possible, to the nearest casualty department and parents will be informed as soon as possible. If this is not the procedure you would like us to follow for your child, please notify us in writing.

Signed: _____ Date: _____

_____

Office Use: Team Colour: _____

filed according to the child's address and the child's name added to the register. If you are using a computer package then the process becomes much easier. By putting the information into a computer program such as Microsoft Access™ then the user is able to retrieve the following:

- An updated register
- A list of children whose birthdays fall that week
- A printout of information sorted according to location of their house
- A list of children who are eligible to join the youth programme

Someone who is computer-literate will need to set up the appropriate templates that allow this information to be retrieved, but once it is up and running inputting the information and getting the necessary documents out should be fairly straightforward even to the most computer-illiterate.

There is a reason for the information being sorted by child's address. A couple of days before the next children's club it is useful to visit the children in their homes. If the children's club is large then the visits need to be divided between several people.

TIP

Don't keep changing the person responsible for visiting a specific area. This is about forming relationships and parents learn to trust a certain face. If we want to build a relationship with the parents that allows open and honest discourse – firstly about the child but later about the gospel in general – then we need to keep the same person knocking on the same door, week in, week out.

Visits will involve many levels of contact. A visit may simply mean knocking on the door and handing over the colouring competition (see Appendix for example) for the following week. As relationships develop it may involve popping in for a cup of tea and a chat. Because I can get away with it, I tell the children that unless I get a biscuit when I knock on their door then I will not hand over the colouring competition – the children know I'm joking (actually it got embarrassing once when a parent came to the door to apologise that she hadn't been shopping yet and there were no biscuits left but could she still have the colouring competition). The reverse of the colouring competition may be used to carry information about your club, but it may also carry information about your church services, counselling information, contact phone number for the minister, etc.

Visiting achieves a lot, and here are some examples:

- It gives parents a chance to express concerns about the children's club. If they didn't get that chance to express concern then they might simply stop their child attending
- It gives you a chance to express your concerns about the child to the parent face to face
- It allows relationship and trust to develop. In one study, 8 out of 10 people said they would consider coming to church if someone they knew invited them, but they would not come if a stranger invited them*
- It reminds the child that the children's club is on. Children often resemble goldfish in the memory department
- It reminds the parent that the children's club is on. Parents often resemble their children who resemble goldfish in the memory department
- It allows you the opportunity to invite the parents to wider church activities from time to time, for example, Alpha, Easter services and Christmas carol services

Without visitation, most children's club attendance charts look like this:

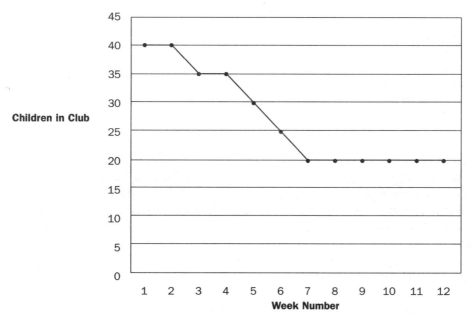

ATTENDANCE WITHOUT VISITS

Children in Club / Week Number

* Statistic supplied by Saddleback Community Church

With home visits our attendance charts could look like this:

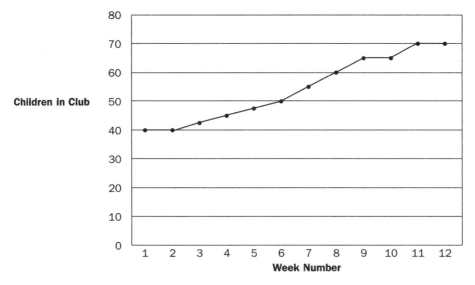

ATTENDANCE WITH VISITS

Because of the work we do before we open clubs, we usually start with a fairly large number. We have visited the school, we have sent a mailshot to all our contacts, we have advertised where possible and we may even have given an incentive for children to come, for example a free chocolate bar. However, from then on we just accept the number of children who come, forgetting all the work that was necessary for high attendance in the first place!

COMMENT

At our Friday night children's project the attendance usually starts at 80 and grows to just over 120 through the term, with the occasional blip for school discos and blizzards! Then it breaks through the 200 mark for the Christmas and Easter specials.

We tackle the situation on two levels:

1. We visit each child who attends. We do this every week.

2. We repeat the processes every week that gave us the high attendance for the first week: we advertise, we may offer an incentive, we visit the school.

Children who live further away from the church should be sent the colouring competition by post. If the information is put into a good database it is not difficult to produce mailing labels.

By the time the child attends for week 2, their name should be on the register. At the end of the academic year, spend some time cleaning up your database. Make sure the youth department has been given the names and addresses of the children eligible to move up. Delete the names of children who've moved out of the area. Delete the names of children who you know will no longer be attending for whatever reason.

If an accident or an incident takes place during the children's club, it must be recorded. Let's stop quickly and define those words:

Accident: This is when something happens of a medical nature, from a splinter right through to concussion

Incident: Any other unfortunate event which isn't covered by "accident". A fight, a child wetting himself, etc.

Record the information on a sheet of paper in a duplicating book. You are going to ask the parent to sign to say that they have seen it, and they will be given a copy to keep. The written record is not intended to be an essay or a thesis. It needs to contain:

What happened   eg John ran into another boy**
What action was taken eg a cold compress was placed on his head
Any follow-up needed   eg keep an eye on him but he wasn't concussed

---

TIP

Keep a personal log. Social Services and associated departments always look for written "evidence". If a parent is unhappy with the way you dealt with something, then write down what they said to you and your response to it. If there are young people giving you difficulties and you have to deal with it, make sure you have written it down. This is your personal log. Nobody else (other than appropriate club staff) should be allowed to see it, only the appropriate authority.

You will need parental permission for practically everything you do. If you are doing face painting then parents will usually have to sign a form ahead of time giving permission for this; if you intend to go on an outing then you will be committing an offence if you take any child outside your building and grounds without a signed consent form from the parents. These rules and regulations shouldn't stop us doing fun and wholesome activities, but we do need to think through all the implications before we go ahead. It is worth developing a registration form that covers the more common activities on site.

If you take your children on an outing then the relevant authorities will expect you to have done a risk assessment and to have taken any necessary measures to reduce the risk.

All this can sound quite hard work. It really isn't. Because of these simple rules and regulations many schools have opted not to take their children on field trips, their view being that it is easier to stay in the school than wade through the red tape. In my opinion the children suffer because of this.

For example: On our summer camp we have an assault course. One of the pieces of apparatus has a rope swing. The child stands on one platform, takes the rope, swings across to the other platform. We look at the apparatus and ask some questions:

1. **Is the physical material safe?** Are the rope and platform safe? Yes. *(If not, will a couple of nails and a hammer solve it?)*
2. **What could happen, what is the risk?**

** We never mention the name of the other child. Parents always find it out, but never from us.

    i. *A child could fall off the rope into the mud below*
    ii. *A child could miss the platform*
    iii.*A child could get on the rope incorrectly*

3. **How do we minimise these risks?**
    i. *A leader stands near the mud*
    ii. *A leader stands on the other platform*
    iii.*A leader shows the child how to hold the rope*

4. **Is the risk minimised enough to use this apparatus?**
    This is your judgement call. When I run our camp I am now satisfied that the risk is minimised enough to use the equipment. The group that come the week after I have finished using the site do not use the rope swing. They went through the same process and concluded the risk was still too great.

Remember, you don't remove the risk – you minimise it. Could a child still fall and hurt themselves? Yes, but the risk is slight. It has never happened in all the years that we have used the camp. There has never been an injury to a child on the rope swing. That's not to say that I and several other adults haven't hurt ourselves, but that is a different story – but I believe with all my heart that one day I will land that rope swing on the other platform on a semi-circle run without hitting the jolly tree!

This is the process for risk assessment on all our activities. You may want to take it a stage further and write down your conclusions, but this is not strictly necessary in most cases.

Don't wrap the children up in cotton wool. Life is about calculated risk-taking. We lose something if we stay inside all the time because it's safer!

COMMUNITY EVENTS AND CHURCH PLANTING

I recently stood in a Bible college which trains the ministers for a particular denomination and asked them the following question:

If 80% of our churchgoers become Christians before they are 18 then why do we concentrate most of our evangelism on those outside this age group? And why don't we rethink the whole thing and plant some children's churches that will grow into youth churches that will grow into fully formed family churches?

After the look of abject horror, some answers began to emerge:

- Existing leaders will not accept it
- It's not financially viable
- It's never been done like that
- It won't work
- It's not biblical
- It undermines the concept of family

Interestingly enough, some of these same objections were thrown at Jesus. Some of them need to be dumped instantly. What other people think of us should never be our motivation. Paul made it very clear:

> *Do you think I am trying to please people? If I were doing that, I would not be a servant of Christ.* (Galatians 1:10)

So is it possible? There are now some very significant churches around that started life as children's clubs. Clearly, it has been done. The programme outlined in "From Alpha to Omega" is designed to show you how to start a children's club within your church. However, it has been constructed in such a way as to make it "freestanding" for those God calls in this direction. By freestanding I don't mean without covering or affiliation. Churches can be built from children's clubs, but these children's clubs must have a line of accountability and covering that runs back to a local church which can provide input, advice, teaching, training and fellowship for leaders.

Paul is one of the best examples of an apostle, and he gives us an insight into the apostolic heart when he writes "I long to plant on virgin soil". There are countless housing estates, city centre blocks of flats and other urban developments that will not be reached by a normal church plant. The parents in these places may never respond. Does this mean we ignore the children? We have an opportunity to change life patterns, to grab hold of a downward spiral and bring the gospel of Christ. Will these parents allow their children to attend children's club? Yes! For some reason there is still a positive residual effect. Parents believe that these clubs will do their children good. I happen to agree with them. Let's consider planting some.

Whether we choose to plant "stand-alone" children's clubs or we start our children's club in the church itself, reaching parents is still an important part of the process. I've listed some ideas that will enable you to do this. The list is not exhaustive; it's intended to give you some ideas that you can develop, so use your imagination:

Parents' Meal with Children's Talent Show

Produce nice invitations and tell the children to invite their parents, their grannies and whomever else they know. Entrance should be by ticket only and the price of the ticket should just cover your costs, unless it is a fundraiser as well, in which case it should include the profit margin you are looking for.

Children are always keen to show off and this gives them the perfect opportunity. Make it a candlelit meal and ask the children to dress in black trousers/skirts and white shirt if they are serving. Escort the parents to their table, play background music, go for it! After dessert and coffee the children will perform. This is a fabulous way of introducing parents to your building. And to make it more effective, make sure your tables contain a mixture of people who already come to your church and people who don't.

One final note of warning: make sure you've seen the talent show items before the talent show. Many a good children's worker has come unstuck because of this!

Family Fun Day

From 10am until 2pm. Bouncy castles are always the key to making life easy, but set the day up as if it were a fairground: coconut shies, leaders in stocks, throw the ball through the hole, penalty shoot-out area, a soft play area for toddlers, face painters, maybe a children's entertainer on hand. A barbecue is essential, and maybe even some candyfloss. Make invites freely available to forthcoming church services. Visit a fairground and let your imagination run riot.

Barn Dance

This still works. Parents will come out to a barn dance and, because of the nature of barn dancing, everyone gets to meet everyone else. It is a splendid way for people to meet others. However it is worth getting a general feel for prospective attendance beforehand. An empty barn dance is rarely a successful event.

Barbecue and Entertainer

The end of the summer term is excellent for this particular activity. Invite all the parents to the end-of-term family barbecue. The first 45 minutes will be taken up by a children's entertainer who will do clowning, illusions and general entertainment for the children. The second 45 minutes or possibly longer will be the barbecue. Persuade the entertainer to stay until the end. He can wander freely amongst the crowd doing balloon modelling, plate spinning, etc. Hire a bouncy castle. Play background music.

Specials

If you are able to get special performers to come to your venue these are prime times to ensure you have invited all the parents and the wider community. The African Children's Choir recently did a tour of the UK and were looking for places to perform in – check out their website and look into booking them in the future; they will pack any venue they perform in. If you can't get the African Children's Choir then maybe organise your own All Nations' Event and invite those from various ethnic backgrounds to come and perform.

WARNING

All of these events work most effectively in the context of established relationships. Parents who have been visited on a regular basis are more likely to attend; people with whom you have developed a relationship are more likely to attend your church services if you invite them. It's all about forming honest and authentic relationships.

Sports Evening

Hold a sports evening for the children and invite the parents to come and watch. Hold the usual parents' races and give prizes. The only caution here is to ensure that some of the parents don't get over-competitive; some parents have come to blows over the outcome of the egg-and-spoon race!

Hire a Local Swimming Pool

Hire the local swimming pool for the evening and invite all the parents of the children who attend your activities. Make a special point on this one that children are not allowed to come alone; they must come with a parent or guardian and not by themselves. If children come by themselves you may have all sorts of problems with child-to-adult ratios in the water. At the end of the night maybe do hot chocolate and chips back at the church.

Pantomime or Musical

If you have the time and the talent then maybe put together a musical or a pantomime for the wider community to come and view. Several years ago we presented *Joseph and The Amazing Technicolor Dreamcoat* and over 500 people from our community came to see the production. As an extension to this idea, invite members of the community to become part of the production as actors, technical people, costume-makers, caterers, etc. The sense of friendship developed in producing live performances can easily be translated to attendance in church. Once again, relationship is the key.

All-age Worship

Many ministers approach the idea of the all-age worship service with great trepidation. It is true to say that, done badly, the all-age service is a nightmare, but done well it is an excellent outreach tool. There are many publications that will provide insights into putting together an all-age worship, but suffice it to say here that from time to time inviting all the families that you have contact with to an all-age service is a good way of familiarising them with the church and the people who attend. The first visit is often the hardest, and once people have taken that step they may be more inclined to come back.

Christingle

This event could not be omitted. It is a wonderful way of drawing in huge numbers of families. Christingle is a custom which originated in the Moravian Church in 1747. It involves children making a Christingle using an orange, some sweets, a candle, some ribbon and a few cocktail sticks. I've enclosed a sketch of a Christingle, but for comprehensive information you will need to go to the Children's Society web page on **www.the-childrens-society.org.uk** and look at the detail. The service takes place on Christmas Eve at approximately 4 or 5pm and lasts for one hour. It is perfect for parents who want to do something with their children before Christmas Eve dinner and early bedtime! If publicised well this service should result in a packed church, with a further opportunity to advertise all your Christmas and New Year services. The advertising could take the form of a leaflet to the local primary schools that explains the significance of the Christingle and provides instructions on how to make one. The children could even bring their own Christingle with them on the evening. Instructions and even order of service are all available on the Children's Society web page.

Prayer Corners

This is a wonderful idea that I have recently stumbled across. The four corners of the church are decorated with items around a certain theme, for example:

Easter: corner 1 – bread and wine
          corner 2 – the cross
          corner 3 – a picture of an empty tomb
          corner 4 – a bottle of perfume, some spilt so that it can be smelt

The children are then split into four groups and travel around each of the four corners, listening to the story of each of the corners as they arrive and then doing an appropriate activity – drawing a picture of bread and wine, etc.

Other ideas for corners include feasts, stations of the cross (type this into an Internet search site if you don't know what the stations are) and Christmas.

Open Night

Parents are often curious about what goes on at the children's club. Hold an open night where parents can come and stand at the back and watch what goes on. Maybe involve them in some of the games. Don't water down your presentation for this evening, for two reasons:

1. It is right and proper that parents get to see exactly what you teach their children
2. Your presentation to children may win some parents to Jesus; it will not be the first time this has happened

End every event with something like the following:

"It has been great to see you all here this evening and I trust you enjoyed yourselves. Just to let you know that MYCHURCH is primarily a church. It exists to let people know that God loves them. We have a church meeting here tomorrow at 11am and every Sunday at the same time, and you are very welcome to attend. Again, thank you for coming and we hope to see you very soon."

Try to have a flyer advertising your next event for people to take away with them. On the back should be a list of your regular church activities and a contact number for enquiries. *You will be surprised how many calls you receive from people who only ever came to one of your events but when they hit a crisis it's your church they call.*

Do not preach on these occasions unless it becomes very natural to do so; do not make appeals; do not become fanatical. These are just awareness events. They are designed to let people see you in a non-threatening atmosphere, to begin to understand that Christians can be fairly normal too – well, most of them!

Please allow me to make a closing comment regarding involvement in the community. It would seem that some churches and ministers will only consider community initiatives and involvement if ultimately they lead to increased church attendance. Whilst I am very keen to propagate community activities that achieve this, I think if we are involved in our communities and cities and towns only for the purpose of winning people to our congregation then we have missed something very important. God called us to be salt and light. He called us to shine in dark places. We should work in our communities to make them better because we want our communities to be better. We should provide safe play environments because play is a good thing and safety is a good thing. We should support community initiatives even if they do not directly benefit us because they benefit our communities. We must move towards a much more holistic view of what we do and why we do it.

We once had a very interesting child attend one of our after-school projects. He had been fostered and the foster parents were considering adoption. The only problem was that the child was wild! We had just fitted a light-blue carpet in the church hall (why light-blue I will never know – I am beginning to suspect that church councils have no idea what church buildings are actually for). We had just started snack time, which happened to involve tomato soup. He was enjoying it by splashing it everywhere. One of the leaders asked him to eat properly. He responded by throwing the tomato soup at the leader. Unfortunately the leader managed to avoid the soup, which landed all over the new carpet (it would have been much easier to clean up the leader than to clean up the new carpet and explain to the church council what had happened). The options were clear. We could keep this child or ask him to leave the project. We knew a little of the background (the first five years of his life before Social Services rescued him could only be described as a living hell) and we kept the child. He was not from one of our church families. He didn't become a regular attendee at our children's club. But we chose to keep him. We later discovered that one of the main reasons that the family had chosen to adopt him and not return him to care was that *we* had chosen to keep him on in the after-school club. Has he become a member of the church? No. Has the family? No. Did we make a difference? Did we positively affect our community and our world? Absolutely! Did it make a difference to that little boy? Absolutely! You see the point: this is not about church attendance; this is about the Kingdom of God being manifest in an expression of love, joy and peace in the Holy Spirit.

SMALLER GROUPS AND THE SUNDAY MORNING CHILDREN'S PROGRAMME

This is all well and good but we have 20 children at our club and our entire village has only 30 children, so how can we outwork what we have just read?

My wife is 65 and I'm 70. We run a children's club for a dozen children each week; some of the things mentioned in this book seem unattainable to us.

In a small church in Scotland in the 1800s the elders gathered for a special meeting. The subject under consideration was the future of their minister. He was getting quite old and the only work of any significance he had undertaken in the last year was to run a Sunday school in which a nine-year-old boy had made a decision to serve Jesus. It didn't take the elders long to reach their decision. The minister was asked to step down.

They did not understand the significance of that little Sunday school and the impact that little boy would have. Don't be discouraged by your small group. *Be encouraged that you are doing what God has called you to do and, although you may never see it, the impact of your ministry will have eternal significance. You will touch the future.*

The little boy grew up. His name was Robert Moffatt, and he is regarded as the founder of modern missions. In one address in an English university he said this:

"There is a land in the North of Africa that has never been reached with the gospel. I saw the smoke of a thousand villages that have never heard the gospel. Who will go?"

A young man in the audience answered in his heart, "I will go". And he did. His name was David Livingstone. Africa owes much to that Scottish minister who did nothing of apparent significance that year, only leading a nine-year-old child to Christ!

There are surprisingly few differences between talking to a small group and to a large group. Let me try and identify the main features that need addressing:

The Incentive System for Reinforcing Positive Behaviour

I find larger groups much easier to control. In the most simplistic sense, by splitting the large group into three teams with a system in place to reinforce positive behaviour and to deter negative behaviour, the groups form into three individuals. The groups control themselves. A child who is talking in a quiet time will be told in no uncertain terms by the rest of the group to stop before he gives points to the other teams. In a small group the individuals remain as individuals and the incentive must be more personal.

For a smaller group consider constructing a star chart (or a more creative alternative). The children should get a star for attendance, another for good behaviour, another for doing their best, another for memorising Bible texts. A small prize may be given at the end of each session or the stars may mount up through the whole term and the winner get a large prize. You may be concerned that this becomes a little competitive. Maybe give a prize to everyone who has five stars or more, but give one big prize to the overall winner – this way, everyone wins.

The Degree of Interaction Changes

To communicate well to a smaller group will involve talking to individuals and getting feedback. Involvement is a key to communication in groups of all sizes, but it is incredibly important with smaller groups. Keep them involved by asking them questions, asking them to hold objects for object lessons, involve them as characters in stories, and keep keeping them involved.

The Relationship Dynamic Changes

Consider the points we made earlier:

- If they do not like you, they will not listen to you
- If you will not listen to them, they will not listen to you
- If you will not have fun with them, they will not listen to you

Now multiply these factors by 100 and you begin to understand smaller-group-relationship dynamics.

With smaller groups the need for regular outings and fun times increases greatly. You have the opportunity for much greater input into their lives; you have the opportunity to *show* them Jesus in you as well as tell them about the Jesus in you.

Some of the most fruitful children's workers work only with small groups. They understand the significance of pouring themselves into a few. Interestingly and rather obviously, Jesus chose to work with small groups.

Ever heard of Edward Kimball? I hadn't until recently. But this man is a hero who started a dazzling line of ministers. Edward Kimball worked with children and in 1858 he led a young boy named Dwight to Jesus. Dwight grew up to be known as D.L. Moody; Moody led a young man named F.B. Meyer to Jesus; F.B. Meyer was to lead J.W. Chapman to Jesus; Chapman led Billy Sunday to Jesus; Billy Sunday led Mordecai Hamm to Jesus, and Hamm in his turn led Billy Graham to Jesus. Don't worry about numbers: win children to Jesus!

What about the Sunday Morning Children's Programme?

Some definitions are needed: by Sunday morning children's programme we are talking about that activity that takes place on Sunday mornings when the adults are in their meeting. It is usually relatively short (unless you happen to be taking the group when an over-enthusiastic preacher is on). The children who attend will be primarily from Christian families.

This section is included because of its importance to the overall picture. A survey of those who had recently joined a new church cited *the quality of the Sunday morning children's ministry as the second most important thing they looked for when seeking to join a church* (number one was the quality of the preaching). Don't skip over that statistic. If your Sunday morning children's provision is not good then people are consciously choosing to go to a different church because of this.

The whole programme must work together. Children who start attending your outreach club, who make decisions for Jesus, who bring their families along on Sunday will now go to the Sunday morning children's programme. So is the Sunday morning children's programme about babysitting? Yes! Should our attitude when we come to teach this group be one of babysitting? Absolutely not!

Don't get hung up on this; you must see the balance. There must be an element of babysitting. We should be caring for children in a safe and secure environment whilst their parents listen to the preaching. Our room, our staffing, our environment, our safety procedures should all reflect the best babysitting service in the world. However, our teaching and our communication must reflect a heartfelt desire to use every single opportunity given to us to win and disciple boys and girls for Jesus.

This chapter should not be read in isolation; many of the programme items outlined in the outreach club format will fit perfectly well here. The time issue obviously doesn't allow for the play element, but the chapters on leaders and vision remain particularly apposite. But there are some issues which are unique to this area and it is to these that we will turn our attention:

How Do We Split the Ages?

This can be quite a challenge. You could have everything from 0 to 14 (children older than 14 should be encouraged to stay in the service, or be working as junior leaders). The education system has already done the majority of the work for us, so the split I suggest is:

0	to 3s	...	Crèche
3	to 4s	...	Pre-School Group
5	to 11s	...	Primary School Group
11	to 14s	...	Secondary School Group

Probably the first task is to rename the groups as something a little more dynamic than "Pre-School Group"! And at the same time a name for the whole programme may be useful. This will give the group an identity. But caution is needed: names that incorporate "school" send out the wrong message; names such as "Junior Church" are simply theologically unsound – the children's gathering represents church – there is no such thing as a junior version.

The previous chapters have already outlined my feelings on the need for a team of people working in each of the groups rather than one person sat on a seat, but let me re-emphasise that to sit one person on a seat with a specific age group is not only ineffective, it is also contrary to most churches' child-protection policies. The younger the age groups the more critical this becomes. In the pre-school group it may be necessary to take the children to the toilet; in the crèche it may become necessary to change nappies. Your workers must be checked by the Criminal Records Bureau and no group should ever be staffed by only one person.

When Do the Children Go to Their Children's Programme Slot?

Do the children go straight to their groups and not join with the adults at all? Do they go to their groups every week?

When my children's friends come to visit, my house seems to split very naturally into age groups. The children play in the playroom or in one of the bedrooms. I am very happy about this, as I work with children much of the time and it is sometimes a delight to be left in a room by myself. However much that I love my moments of solitude (increasingly rare though they are), my children will never learn anything from me if I keep them in a separate room all the time. It is very important that the children see adults worshipping. It is vitally important that at least once a quarter children stay in for the whole service and that the service takes on an "all-age flavour".

What Should the Format of the Morning Children's Programme Be?

There is a limited period of time, but I still suggest using a condensed version of the Children's Programme outline listed in the "Alpha to Omega" section. Start the sessions with prayer and children's praise songs. Because the songs cut across the age groups it is good to have the 3- and 4-year-olds mixed in with the 5 to 11s for the singing. After 10–15 minutes of prayer and songs the 3- and 4-year-olds move off to their group. The 11 to 14s go straight to their group – with all the hormones flying around this group it is probably best to send them to the youth specialists as soon as possible!

Use whatever incentive is appropriate to the size of the group, but a positive reinforcement method should be used.

What Teaching Materials Do We Use?

The prayer, praise, games, etc format advocated in a later section should be used at the start of the programme, but the second section – the teaching programme – could be taken from countless publications, and there are many options, as you will see if you visit your local Christian bookshop. The material that suits your group is the best material to use. You may need to experiment. Options include:

- *Salt* produced by Scripture Union
- *Adventurers* produced by CPAS
- *Roots*
- *Living Stones* written by Susan Sayers

● *Fusion* and *Impact* by Mark Griffiths (although not written for this particular setting, these books are being used in this context to good effect).

TIP

Give every child a treasure box or scrap book. Each week give the children an item related to that week's story to place in their book or box. This will help with continuity of attendance. Children will not want to miss out on that week's item for their box or book.

And Finally: Keep the Profile of Children's Ministry High on the Church's Agenda

● The presiding minister should pray for the children and the children's leaders as they leave for their groups
● The children should have the opportunity to sing their songs in front of the adults regularly
● At least once a year the church's vision for young people and children should be presented to the whole church
● The church council should allocate a reasonable budget to the children's programme

The Level Way
Above Average

YOU JUST HAVE TO KEEP GOING

David had been journeying long and hard. He had led his men valiantly. He had lived with incredible standards of integrity and righteousness. He had always done the right thing. Yet he had just returned from the journey, hoping to come back to his wife and children, hoping for a time of rest and relaxation before he had to continue on. Then suddenly as he rode into camp he saw smoke billowing high into the air. It was his camp. Ziklag was on fire. His possessions were in flames. As he came closer the enormity of the situation hit him. Not only were all his possessions on fire, but his wife and children and everything he and his men owned were gone.

And, as if the situation could possibly get any worse, now his friends, those he had helped, those he had encouraged when they were downcast and depressed, those whom he had carried when they couldn't support themselves – those self-same men now wanted to kill him; they wanted to stone their leader to death.

David was facing one of his bleakest moments; he had entered a dark time – a time that we are not immune from, a defining moment in his life. Several weeks after this episode David would ride triumphantly into Jerusalem and be crowned king. He would prove to be the greatest king Israel would ever have apart from King Jesus himself. But before he gets to Jerusalem, he must get through Ziklag.

Ziklag is that defining moment which enables us to move onto that level way above average or it can be the moment when we decide that mediocrity is where we will live our lives. It is the central base around which all else hinges. It is David's final test before kingship. If he passes this test then he will walk on into triumph and glory; if he fails this test the shepherd boy will at best return to his sheep, or at worst he will die.

David's past was incredibly exciting. He had been anointed king by Samuel the prophet, and he had defeated Goliath. He had gathered to himself men and women who were depressed, discouraged, in debt and desperate, and David had made them great. But now he faces the defining moment.

We all come there. We must. Anyone worth anything in God's kingdom must pass the Ziklag test. They must prove faithful under intense pressure; they must have sufficient strength that they don't shrink away at the first sign of opposition. Allow me to make some general observations on David's predicament that may help us also:

1. **The decision was his** – God willed him to get up and sort out the situation – but he would never override his special gift to mankind, he would never override free will. The decision here was David's and David's alone
2. **He was on his own,** nobody was going to help him up
    i. He had no physical support – his men were not going to support or help him, on the contrary they wanted to kill him
    ii. He had no material support – all his material possessions had been taken
    iii. He had no emotional support – his wife and children had been taken away, his emotional shelter was gone

It so happens that there isn't always someone there to help you up, and sometimes God designs it that way. Stripped of everything, what will David do?

3. **Those he had worked with,** those he had strengthened and encouraged now wanted to stone him. Anyone who has ever held a position of responsibility will understand the emotions that this brings up

I genuinely believe that we must all face that place of Ziklag, that place where two different futures open up before us. And for everyone who comes through to be a king I wonder how many return to being shepherds. Having destiny is not enough; being prophesied over is not enough. Many people have destiny but may never see it fulfilled.

It would be true to say that 90% of our life is governed by our decisions and only 10% by unforeseen circumstances. However, I think it is our response and our decision process within the 10% that define us, that decision in the unforeseen circumstance, that decision when we feel devoid of everything, that decision in the ZIKLAG time that makes the difference.

The times when nobody wants to support our vision to reach boys and girls for Jesus, that time when nobody wants to work with us, that time when we are physically and emotionally drained. Dragging ourselves out week after week, through those cold autumnal evenings and those depressing winter nights to do what we are convinced God called us to do. And to learn that in those times it is God himself who destines us to be devoid of support and of those who would encourage us does not help. But it is so important that God allows us to go through these times, for ultimately it is the builder who defines the shape of the building. If God can get his builders right then there is no real issue when it comes to what they build. Paul built as a wise master builder. It was going to be good and healthy and full of God because that was what Paul was like. The builder defines the shape.

And David was always going to prove himself at Ziklag. Sun Tze, the ninth-century Chinese general, commented in his book *The Art of War* that victories are won before the battles begin. And David had been through many tests that prepared him for Ziklag. At the time the other tests must have seemed difficult, but they all prepared the man of God for the next rung of the ladder. So let's see what we can learn from David:

1. **He had an open and honest relationship with God**

   David wasn't just praying liturgical prayers that he had memorised; David had cultivated an open and honest relationship with the creator of the universe. He told God how he felt.

2. **He knew about the power of praise**

   Psychologists are only just beginning to realise the potential of music to change our moods and emotions. David knew more than this. He knew that God himself inhabited the praise of his people and through praise he could lift his feelings, his emotions and his spirit and position himself to overcome in every situation.

3. **He knew how to draw power from outside himself**

   New-Age gurus talk of our need to draw power from within, to draw strength from something mystical inside us. (It is almost certainly a distortion of the Ecclesiastes teaching that eternity has been hidden in our hearts). But David knew that it wasn't mystical power from within that he needed, but instead supernatural power from without. He needed to draw strength from his God as he had done so many times in the past.

If we can build these principles very firmly into our lives BEFORE THE BATTLE – then we will always be successful and live our lives on a level way above average. Let us remember the sobering thought that for every person who goes on to be king there are many who return to being a shepherd. To change this generation of boys and girls we desperately need some people who will operate on a level way above average and I believe that God is raising those people up right now. But they must pass through Ziklag.

Catherine Booth was the wife of General William Booth, the founder of the Salvation Army. Catherine was struggling with the idea of joining her husband as he travelled throughout the UK and beyond to share the gospel. Catherine had seen William being verbally and physically abused as he stood outside public houses preaching. She saw bottles thrown at him and the constant torment that he endured as he saw men and women won to Jesus. Catherine decided to commit the whole thing to God in prayer, so she knelt and began to pray.

The account says that as she prayed Jesus himself appeared before her in a vision. She asked Jesus if there was another way. Jesus held up his nail-pierced hands as if to indicate that sometimes his way was a way of suffering. Catherine bowed her head and then asked:

"Then, Lord, will you be with me?"

Jesus answered:

"Until the end of time."

In the strength of these words Catherine stood and joined her husband, boldly proclaiming the gospel.

Sometimes to follow Jesus involves sacrifice and suffering. There never was a guarantee that it would be easy, but if we can keep going and build the right principles into our lives and never give up then we can make amazing things happen and we have a promise from Jesus himself:

I will be with you always, even until the end of the world. (Matthew 28:20)

CLIMBING EVEREST

There is an excellent story about a Mafia boss who wanted a minister to bury his brother. The boss had gone to all the churches throughout the town, asking the minister at each one to bury his brother. They had all refused. The Anglicans, the Baptists, the Methodists, the Unitarians, the Lutherans. He had tried them all and they all said no. Eventually he found a small, independent church just outside the town. He said to the minister:

"If you will bury my brother then I will make a donation of $1,000,000 to your church. All I ask is that you say one good thing about my brother."

The minister thought and then, to make sure the Mafia boss was under no misconception, he warned:

"I must tell the truth, you do realise that?"

The boss replied:

"That's fine. All you need to do is say one good thing and the money is yours."

The funeral day came and the church was full of mobsters all wearing sunglasses and suits, with guns clearly bulging underneath. The minister stood to speak. The Mafia boss whispered: "Remember priest, just one good thing and the money is yours."

The minister approached the lectern and began:

"The man who is lying in the coffin was a thief. He killed people. He lied to people. He hurt people. He sold guns."

The congregation became uncomfortable but the priest continued: "He sold drugs. He was not a nice man... "

Then the priest winked at the Mafia boss and the Mafia boss knew that the one nice thing would be next.

"He kidnapped people; he held up banks. He was not a nice man – but, compared to his brother, he was an absolute angel."

Comparisons are always dangerous. If I compare how well my club is doing with the club down the road, I may feel I am doing very well; if I compare my club with the children's works in New York or Mexico City that are attracting 25,000 every week I may feel a sudden case of depression arriving. Comparisons are always dangerous. We must be who God has called us to be and do what God has called us to do, in the place he has called us to.

Having said that, I do believe that we should aim much higher than we presently do. Some of us are aiming at molehills; some of us are aiming at small slopes and even the best among us are only aiming at Snowdon or Ben Nevis. We need to aim at Everest. Why? Because it's there. Because *many of us have the potential to do something that shakes communities, cities and nations, and while our focus remains on the molehill we will never do it.*

Why settle for being the king of a molehill when you can stand on Everest?

If we can begin to grasp afresh what God is really like then it just might catapult us onto a new level of children's ministry. The book of Job gives us some insight.

Job has definitely had some difficulties. God has allowed Satan to strip him of everything except his life. When he started off he was certainly enjoying his own personal summertime. He was rich; he had a family; he had good health. Autumn arrived and things began to be cut off: his wealth, his health, his family. When we reach the end chapters Job is certainly in his own personal winter. He has nothing left; all has been stripped away. He is barely alive. And all is about to come full circle and springtime is on its way and God will begin to restore. But just before God starts to restore, Job makes a mistake, a huge mistake. He questions God.

Let's look at what happens next. Needless to say, Job is in serious trouble. Here are some extracts from the conversation that follows:

> *From out of a storm, the LORD said to Job: Why do you talk so much when you know so little? Now get ready to face me! Can you answer the questions I ask? How did I lay the foundation for the earth? Were you there? Doubtless you know who decided its length and width. What supports the foundation? Who placed the cornerstone, while morning stars sang, and angels rejoiced?* (Job 38:1–7)

> *Did you ever tell the sun to rise? And did it obey?* (Job 38:12)

> *Can you arrange stars in groups such as Orion and the Pleiades? Do you control the stars or set in place the Great Bear and the Little Bear? Do you know the laws that govern the heavens, and can you make them rule the earth? Can you order the clouds to send a downpour, or will lightning flash at your command?* (Job 38:31–35)

I suspect by now Job knows he is in trouble.

> *I am the LORD All-Powerful, but you have argued that I am wrong. Now you must answer me. (Job 40:1–2)*

Then revelation dawns and Job understands afresh who he is dealing with. Note the things he says here:

Job said to the LORD: Who am I to answer you? I did speak once or twice, but never again. (Job 40:3–5)

No one can oppose you, because you have the power to do what you want.

You asked why I talk so much when I know so little. I have talked about things that are far beyond my understanding. You told me to listen and answer your questions. (Job 42:3–4)

I heard about you from others; now I have seen you with my own eyes.
Let us fuse these words into our minds and hearts:

No one can oppose you, because you have the power to do what you want. (Job 42:2)

When Lucy is talking to Mr Beaver in *The Lion, the Witch and The Wardrobe* (C. S. Lewis) she is concerned about all the talk about Aslan the Lion. She asks Mr Beaver:
"Is Aslan a tame lion?"
Mr Beaver responds:
"Oh no, Lucy, Aslan is not a tame lion."
History sometimes passes down to us the concept of a tame God who does what we ask, the puppy-dog God. God is not like this.
For us to run and to be confident that we can stand on Everest we need to understand that the God we serve is compassionate and loving and just and righteous and holy and giving and caring – but he is also powerful and wild and untameable and can easily accomplish that which he has purposed. Let us never forget this.
This is the story of Gladys Aylward (first published in *IMPACT*):
Saturday, October 15, 1932: Gladys Aylward left from Liverpool Street Station in London for the long train ride across Europe and Russia. God had told her to go to China and to China she was going to go.
Gladys Aylward was one of those people who had been touched by God. She knew what it was to have a life touched by Jesus himself. It made her spectacular. She might not have been clever enough to get through college. She might have been told that she would never be able to go to China, but she didn't believe it. She knew who Jesus was and he had changed her life.
People might have said no, but she was going anyway. God had said yes.
Gladys worked at other jobs and saved her money. Then she heard of a 73-year-old missionary, Mrs Jeannie Lawson, who was looking for a younger woman to carry on her work in China. Gladys wrote to Mrs Lawson. Mrs

Lawson told her that if she could make it to China then she could stay with her and work with her. So she set off from London with her passport, her Bible, her tickets, and two pounds, to travel to China.

The journey was far from easy. The first difficulty was travelling through Germany, where the officials were not happy when they asked her why she was going to China and she simply replied:

"God said."

They asked her many questions. They tried to stop her continuing but there was no way this lady was turning back. But the worst was yet to come.

She travelled on through Russia. The Russians were at war with China and the journey was very hazardous. At one point, at a place called Chita, the train stopped and soldiers boarded the train and commanded everyone to get off. But Gladys protested, her ticket said Dairen, a place on the China Sea, and she would not get off until she arrived there. The train continued. But some miles later the train was stopped again and this time the conductor announced that the train would not go any further for several months.

Gladys had no choice but to get off the train and walk back to Chita. It was a long walk and before long the night had come and with it the numbing cold. She stopped to rest under a tunnel. In the background she could hear the sounds of wolves howling in the Russian countryside. Wolves coming closer, but as it turned out the morning came before the wolves and she continued to Chita. At Chita she boarded another train and despite a long argument with another soldier she insisted on being taken to Dairen. The train continued on but no further than Vladivostok.

In Vladivostok the secret police interrogated her and would certainly have locked her in prison if a stranger hadn't helped her escape to the harbour. At the harbour she tried to get on a ship to Japan, but the captain refused to take her because she had no money. She pleaded with him until he agreed to take her.

From Japan to Tientsin, and then by train, then bus, then mule, to the inland city of Yangchen, in the mountainous province of Shansi, a little south of Peking (Beijing). Most of the residents had seen no Europeans other than Mrs Lawson, and now Miss Aylward.

The college principal said NO but God said Yes; the Germans said NO but Gladys kept going because God said Yes; the Russians said NO but Gladys kept going because God said Yes; the wolves tried to stop her but God had said Yes; the secret service tried to stop her but God said Yes; even the China Sea tried to stand in her way, but this was a life touched by God; this was a life that Jesus had made spectacular; nothing would or could stop her.

She would do what God had told her to do. This was a spectacular lady. God was going to do amazing things through this lady. A spectacular life. A life that would never be content on the molehill, this was a life destined for Everest. Gladys stood five feet tall. She was not intelligent by the world's measure of intelligence. She simply did what God had asked. And therein lies the key.

She simply did what God had asked.

And here is Job's second revelation:

I heard about you from others; now I have seen you with my own eyes.
(Job 42:5)

God is looking for children's workers who will have a genuine relationship with him and simply do what he asks. Everest is not about high numbers, although I believe all our clubs should be better attended. Everest is not about higher profile, although again I believe that we are here to make God's name famous. Everest is about doing what God asks. For you, Everest may be 50 children whom you will look after and nurture and disciple; for someone else it may be 5,000 or 50,000. Everest is doing what God asks with an understanding that God is well able to work through you to accomplish his purpose.

For some, Everest might be the "state-of-the-art" children's centre in the heart of your community – a place where children can come and play in safety and security, where they and their parents can learn about a God of love. For others, the rickety shed in the worst housing estate in the country may be your Everest. Everest is what God has asked you to do.

Don't be content with the molehill. Close the molehill, walk away from the molehill, transform the molehill into Everest, but *for the sake of this glorious gospel and to glorify this amazing, all-powerful God, let us never settle for the molehill.*

Finally, keep smiling. It is a staggering revelation to some, but doing what God wants you to do can actually be fun. Being at the very centre of God's will is liberating and empowering. Even in the middle of the fiercest battles it brings great release and security. Enjoy the journey; don't just keep looking for the destination. The late Michael Ramsey, former Archbishop of Canterbury, put it like this:

You have to be serious, but never be solemn, because if you are solemn about anything there is a risk of becoming solemn about yourself.

My friend Doug Horley put it like this:

I will run this race and I will never stop.
Follow Jesus until the day I drop.
I can do all things through Christ who strengthens
me.
When you've got such a lot,
When you've not got a lot.
What? Be happy!

The Beginners' Guide

A→Z

A * FROM ALPHA TO OMEGA * Ω

THE STEP-BY-STEP GUIDE TO ESTABLISHING A THRIVING CHILDREN'S OUTREACH PROGRAMME

The aim of this chapter is to show you how to start a children's club from scratch. It will give you a timescale for activities and, in some cases, expected outcomes. The difficulty with presenting practice is that it doesn't always translate into every situation. Hopefully the preceding chapters will have built in enough principles to allow the discussion of practice. But again the warning: this section is meant to help, not to hinder; it is here as your slave and not your master. Use it, but don't be confined by it.

Before You Start

There are many issues that need to be weighed up before you start an outreach children's club, because once something is up and running it is very hard to change its form or shape. It has always been my preference to start from scratch, as taking over from someone else is always going to be difficult. But I am aware that this is not always a possibility and some diplomatic skills may be needed to re-form an existing club.

The lie: Wait until all the conditions are right before you start

Wait until you have the right staff, wait until you are all experts on the programme, wait until you have all the equipment you need. Forget It! Start. It'll never be the perfect time, but God blesses people on the journey, not while they're waiting for the perfect conditions.

This section contains four parts:

1. The timetable for the first two years
2. The timetable for the usual year
3. The children's club
4. The children's club programme from beginning to end

THE TIMETABLE FOR THE FIRST TWO YEARS

The WHY section is simply a reminder of what has been mentioned in the previous chapters. For a full explanation of WHY, refer to the appropriate chapter.

WHEN	WHAT	WHY
Pre Start	Take some time to pray and understand the area you are working in. If you are new to the area this is particularly important.	God may have a specific key that will enable you to establish the whole thing so much quicker. Give God time to speak to you.
January to July (Year 1)	Make contact with one or more schools and schedule some assemblies.	Schools will be the place the children who attend your club will come from.
January	Begin to share your vision and form your team.	Your ability to reproduce leaders will be the single most important factor in determining the extent of your vision.
February	Begin to think finance. Are there local grant organisations that can help with start-up funding. Are there opportunities for child-based businesses? Can you start an after-schools' project in your building? How about a holiday play scheme in the summer?	Vision will always need *provision.*
April	Send the schools letters advertising assemblies for June and July.	
August	If you have children already linked in, take them to summer camp.	Summer camp is an excellent opportunity to have significant input into your children's lives. It gives you six days away with them.
	Run your holiday play schemes.	A chance to bring in some extra income, but also an opportunity for spiritual input over a week.

September	Start your business opportunity or activate your other sources of income.	
	Begin to advertise your children's club in schools, in shop windows, by word of mouth.	People will not come if they don't know it exists.
	Staff training night. To complement all the informal training nights up until now.	Invest in your team. Give regular training and input.
October	Launch your children's club.	The rubber hits the road! Time to put it all together.
November	Hold a community event – parents' party.	This never was and never will be just about reaching children. This is about winning families.
December	The Christmas special for all the children you now have contact with. Make it a big one, with selection boxes for all those who attend.	The big end-of-year bash will close your first year in style. Make sure ALL your child contacts are invited. Schools, holiday play schemes, children's club.
	Send schools letters for January, February and March assemblies.	Get all your school assembly administration out of the way quickly.
	Send Christmas cards to all your contacts.	It's *always* about relationship.
	Staff/leaders' party.	Work hard but also play hard. Reward your leaders. If at all possible, have a great night together and don't allow them to pay!
January (Year 2)	Restart children's club.	
	Start small groups.	Purposeful discipleship happens best in small groups.

April	The Easter special for all the children you know.	
	If you are starting a church from scratch using the children's work as your start point, then start a Sunday service now. Make Easter Sunday your first service.	
	If no church plant then run a community event here – swimming night maybe, or a family fun day.	
	Don't do any children's activities or schools' work in April; evaluate here.	Don't move into headless-chicken mode. Keep sharp and focused. You achieve this by stopping and evaluating from time to time.
	Send the schools letters advertising assemblies for June and July.	
May	Restart the children's club.	
July	Community event – barbecue with entertainer.	
August	If you have children already linked in, take them to summer camp.	
	Run your holiday play schemes.	
September	Begin to advertise your children's club in schools, in shop windows, by word of mouth.	
	If you started from scratch then start your youth activities now. If you didn't, then ensure your children are making a smooth transition into the youth department.	Children don't stay children for long. They will need to move into a dynamic youth programme eventually.
	Staff training night. To complement all the informal training nights up until now.	

	Send schools letters to advertise assemblies for October to December.	
October	Launch your children's club.	
November	Hold a community event – parents' party.	
December	The Christmas special for all the children you now have contact with. Make it a big one, with selection boxes for all those who attend.	
	Send Christmas cards to all your contacts.	
	Advertise your Christmas services to all your contacts, especially Christingle and Carols by Candlelight.	
	Send schools letters for January, February and March assemblies.	
	Staff/leaders' party.	

THE TIMETABLE FOR THE NORMAL YEAR

January	Start children's club.
	Start small groups for purposeful discipleship.
April	The Easter special for all the children you know.
	Community event here – swimming night maybe.
	Send the schools letters advertising assemblies for June and July.
May	Restart the children's club.
July	Community event – barbecue with entertainer.
August	If you have children already linked in, take them to summer camp.
	Run your holiday play schemes.
September	Begin to advertise your children's club in schools, in shop windows, etc.
	Ensure all your children who are eligible are incorporated into youth group.
	Staff training night.
	Send schools letters to advertise assemblies for October to December.
October	Launch your children's club.
November	Hold a community event – parents' party possibly.
December	The Christmas special for all the children you now have contact with.
	Send Christmas cards to all your contacts.
	Advertise your Christmas services to all your contacts.
	Send schools letters for January, February and March assemblies.
	Staff/leaders' party.

THE CHILDREN'S CLUB

Arrival and departure is important. Have a good register that keeps track of names, addresses and any ailments that you should be aware of. Have a contact number for parents. Talk to parents; allow them to see your face. It's hard for a parent to trust an anonymous name on the bottom of a sheet of paper. It's much easier to trust someone they've seen and met. For this reason, even though teenagers may man various activities and hold positions of responsibility, it is better to place an adult at the reception area.

Charge a small admission fee. The more self-sufficient the club can be, the better. Remember, I am suggesting that these clubs can be the seeds for new churches. Some will need to be completely self-sufficient.

Hall Set-up and Structure

Make the hall as colourful and as child-friendly as possible. You may not be allowed to decorate the building from top to bottom with the latest cartoon characters, but you can still use colourful banners and exciting background music. The hall should be at the appropriate temperature so children don't need to keep their coats on all night. The room should be brightly lit.

Why Three Teams?

If two teams are used then usually there is a winning team and a losing team. Having three teams allows one team to win and the others to come joint second. It allows an element of healthy competitiveness without there needing to be a loser. Other children's groups (some very large groups) work with two teams, one of boys and the other of girls. There are two main disadvantages of this system:

1. There is very rarely an equal mix of boys and girls
2. It leads to unnecessary tension – tension between the teams and also with Social Services, who will frown on the practice. (Wherever possible it will pay you to keep government organisations feeling positive towards your work – Jesus had favour with God AND MEN)

STAFFING

Registration

Three members – This is where you meet the parents. This is the initial contact point. First impressions do last, so put some of your best here. The registration people will also need to be armed with information regarding trips, etc. This is the place to base your administrators.

Welcome Person

An adult or several adults who greet the children on arrival and give a quick guided tour and breakdown of the format to those who are new. This is the place to base your pastors.

Activity Supervisor

Each activity (such as bouncy castle, computers, etc) needs to be supervised by an activity supervisor. This can be one of your teenagers as long as they are prepared to be responsible.

Scores

A competent and upbeat member of the team who will periodically announce the scores. We presently have a person called "Gorgeous Nick" to do the scores – the children's idea, not mine.

Tuck Shop/Café Area

This is fairly self-explanatory, but suffice it to say that the café area does generate finance for the project and give us an opportunity to talk to the children.

Technical

A person who operates PA, videos, OHP, etc is invaluable. If done well this will help you greatly; if done badly this can destroy your programme.

Front People

A front person with the possible addition of a second for illustrations. If you work with two front people who know what they are doing and have obvious communication gifts, then introduce a third who can develop and learn. As they come to maturity in this gift then delegate more to them. This is a continual process and will allow you to move or sow out into other children's works. The choice of the third person is very important. They may not be the most gifted at first, but they must be humble, teachable and have the heart of a servant. Don't choose anyone without these qualifications. The front is the place for your evangelists and teachers and maybe your apostles.

Floaters

The job description is in the title. These people float around checking everyone is OK – talking to children, sitting in the café area with them, chilling with them, getting to know them, caring for them. The people with pastoral gifts and a heart for children thrive in this position.

Others

If you run crafts as part of your programme then you will need artistic people. A qualified first-aider should not be overlooked. Members of the team will also need to be involved in the weekly visiting programme. You may also have a person to be the team leader of each team. Our green team leader is presently Gregory the Green!

During the programme part of the evening there will need to be a sprinkling of leaders in each team. Problems should not be dealt with from the front but sorted out quickly from within the team. For the staff as well as for the children it will be a process of education.

THE CHILDREN'S CLUB PROGRAMME FROM BEGINNING TO END

Because we believe that in order for the children to listen to us we must listen to them, and in order for them to listen to us we must have fun with them, and in order for them to listen to us we must be liked by them, we run the first 45 minutes of our programme with the children being allowed to choose between a range of activities.

Give a quick guided tour to the children who are there for the first time. All the children need to be instructed that on arrival they need to place their coats on the back of the seats that they will later sit on, and that for the first 45 minutes they are free to join whatever activity they like. They may choose from:

- Computers
- Bouncy castle
- Crafts
- Café area
- Outside play (weather and availability of a secure garden allowing)
- Snooker/pool
- Video

They also need to know that they don't have to stay at any of these areas; they may freely move from one to another. Some of the activities are simply there for the children to have fun with; some of the activities are there to allow the children time to speak to leaders – the café area is an example of this.

Crafts

It is always useful to have a good craft activity that relates to the overall theme for the week. Assign a creative person to come up with an idea each week, based on the theme. When the children take things home it helps reinforce the message and at the same time allows a Christian activity into a possibly non-Christian home. Use paints, use glitter, use glass painting, use textiles: be creative.

Outside Sports and Bouncy Castle

Joyfully, the more boisterous children always opt to go to these activities. The activities must therefore be well supervised. I say "joyfully" because it means they are expending energy that might otherwise be used to the disrupt the teaching programme. Bouncy castles, football, basketball, short tennis can all be incorporated according to the space available.

Computer Games

I always have reservations about this area, because children seem to spend so much time at home on computers that it would be nice to give them a change. But it seems that some children initially attended because we had computers that they could use to show off to their friends how good they were at certain games. The club gave them an audience. Because it attracts people to our teaching programme, the computers have stayed.

Timing

After 45 minutes we play a specific piece of music that the children quickly learn to recognise. It is currently "MISSION IMPOSSIBLE"! On hearing the music the children leave their activity and rush to their seats. It may not happen in week 1 or 2, but by week 3 they'll come running. As in all these things, it's a process of education.

Section 2 is for 1 hour and 15 minutes, with the numbers in brackets being maximum running times.

WARNING

The 1989 Children's Act states that if an activity runs for more than 2 hours a week and for more than 5 days a year it must be registered – formerly with Social Services, now with OFSTED. It is important that our clubs are safe places, and where it is possible to police-check our staff we should do so. However, there are many difficulties in registering: there will need to be one toilet for every 8 children; some of our older buildings will need renovation; there is a fee which is payable annually and the big difficulty is that the majority of staff will need a play-worker qualification. My advice is do all that you can to comply with regulations, but stay within the 2 hours so that you do not have to register.

The items of the teaching programme are listed on subsequent pages, but utilise the following format:

	Programme	*Timing* **(this is maximum time for each item)**
Section 1	Welcome	3 minutes
	Rules	2 minutes
	Prayer	5 minutes
	Introductory Praise	7 minutes
	Game 1	5 minutes
	Praise	10 minutes
	Fun Item 1	5 minutes
	Game 2	5 minutes
	Fun Item 2	5 minutes
	Bible Text	3 minutes
	Announcements	2 minutes
	Interview	5 minutes
	Worship Time	10 minutes
Section 2	Bible Lesson	5 minutes
Preaching	Illustration 1	5 minutes
Time	Illustration 2	5 minutes
	Illustration 3	5 minutes
	Story	15 minutes
	Prayer	5 minutes

If each item runs for the maximum time allowed then you have a 107-minute programme. We are aiming for 75 minutes. Obviously each item must not go to the maximum, but it is better to be tight at the end than to finish 15 minutes early!

⇨ Welcome (3 minutes)
This is a chance to welcome the children, but also an opportunity to have fun with them. Remember: if you will not have fun with them, they will not listen to you. I prefer to lead the programme with others at the front, eg the score person, team leaders, your trainee leader. This allows comical banter between the leaders. Think differently! Walk on dressed as Barney™ and welcome the children. Be creative.

⇨ Rules (2 minutes)
If there are no clear rules then the children have no disciplinary guidelines, and cannot be reprimanded for not obeying rules that they have never heard. Only two simple rules are necessary:

● Nobody leaves their seat. If they need to go to the toilet then they must put their hand up and ask permission from a leader to go
● When the whistle blows everyone stops speaking, sits down, focuses on the front and makes no sound. If you are uncomfortable with the use of a whistle, you can use a horn, or a special word

These two simple rules will keep everything controlled. Children feel safer and more secure in a disciplined atmosphere. There must be a method of enforcing the rules. We use the following two-fold system:

Positive Enforcement
If a team is particularly good, ie the members sit well, listen well, or cheer the loudest, they win a game. Then they get to roll the dice. The score from the dice is added to their overall score. The team with the most points at the end of the term gets the biggest prizes; the other teams also receive prizes, but lesser ones. For example, at the end of the Easter term the winning team will receive an Easter Egg and the other teams a cream egg.

	Programme
Section 1	Welcome
	Rules
	Prayer
	Introductory Praise
	Game 1
	Praise
	Fun Item 1
	Game 2
	Fun Item 2
	Bible Text
	Announcements
	Interview
	Worship Time
Section 2	Bible Lesson
Preaching	Illustration 1
Time	Illustration 2
	Illustration 3
	Story
	Prayer

Negative Enforcement

If a child talks after the whistle has gone or is not sitting and facing the front, then they instantly lose six points from their score.

TIP

You don't have to bring prizes every week. If you keep a running score for each team you can inform them that they are working towards the best score for the end of term, when the team that comes first will receive the largest selection box/Easter egg, and the other two teams will receive small selection boxes/Easter eggs. Also, the age-old tactic of rewarding those who attend most often with attendance prizes at the end of term will ensure that you don't get the spasmodic attendance common to many children's clubs up and down the country.

⇨ **Prayer (5 minutes)**

In two sections:

1. *Giving Thanks*

   Children who have prayed for something the week before (or several weeks before) and whose prayers have been answered should be asked to come and tell the others how God answered their prayer.

2. *Bringing Needs*

   Some of the children will want to pray for certain things. Allow them to come and mention what they are praying for and ask God together to answer prayer.

Remember, when children have prayers answered they need to be invited to the front to give God thanks.

⇨ **Longer Prayer Nights (15 minutes)**

Some nights you may wish to hold an extra-long prayer session. You can do this in several ways:

		Programme
Section 1	Welcome
	Rules
	Prayer
	Introductory Praise
	Game 1
	Praise
	Fun Item 1
	Game 2
	Fun Item 2
	Bible Text
	Announcements
	Interview
	Worship Time
Section 2	Bible Lesson
Preaching	Illustration 1
Time	Illustration 2
	Illustration 3
	Story
	Prayer

P.R.A.Y.

The four corners of the building are given the letters P, R, A and Y respectively. If there are more than 40 children then the centres will also need to be used, as follows:

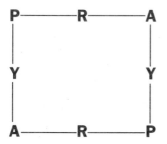

A leader is placed at each base and the children are split into four groups (eight for above). The children start at one of the bases, but will remain there for only two minutes. After two minutes they will move clockwise to the next base. The bases are:

P for Praise

At this base the children will stand in a circle and give thanks for one thing which is good in their lives. "God, thank you for my family"; "God thank you for the children's club"; "God, thank you that I'm healthy." If they visit another P base then the leader may simply talk them through all the things we have to be thankful for: salvation, creation, life, eternal life.

R is for Repent

At this base the children will be reminded by the base leader that all of us have done things wrong, things that hurt God. This would be a good time to think quietly about things we have done wrong that hurt God and maybe ask God to forgive us.

A is for Ask

At this base one or two children might lead in prayer and ask God for a good night, or maybe a safe journey home at the end; or maybe there are specific requests for relatives who are sick.

	Programme
Section 1	Welcome
	Rules
	Prayer
	Introductory Praise
	Game 1
	Praise
	Fun Item 1
	Game 2
	Fun Item 2
	Bible Text
	Announcements
	Interview
	Worship Time
Section 2	Bible Lesson
Preaching	Illustration 1
Time	Illustration 2
	Illustration 3
	Story
	Prayer

Y is for Yourself

At this base the children will be encouraged to ask God for something for themselves. Give them quick guidance on what sort of things, but allow the children to ask God to bless them, or to give them a good night at children's club.

From time to time children will spend their Ask and their Yourself time asking God to let their team win. Don't be worried by this; I'm not sure if God has ever got involved in the scoring system at children's club.

Walk

Send the children to walk around the building on the outside. Send a leader first and after he has travelled 5 metres, send the first child. His instructions are simple:

1. He is going to walk and talk to God in the same way that he might walk and talk to a friend, he is going to tell God how he feels and what is bothering him etc.
2. He is never going to lose sight of the person in front
3. He is never going to catch up with the person in front, there will always be a 5 metre gap.

When the child has gone 5 metres send the next, until all the children have gone. This calls for close supervision and we need to send adults in between every five or six children.

Circles

- Ask the children to find a space. In the space ask them to talk to God about themselves for one minute
- After one minute the children get together with another child and they pray for each other. They put their hands on each other's shoulders and in turn pray something like: "God, help my friend learn more about you"
- After one minute the two join with another two and pray in their four that God will give them a good night
- After one minute the four join with another four and pray that God will look after their families – or something similar

	Programme
Section 1	Welcome
	Rules
	Prayer
	Introductory Praise
	Game 1
	Praise
	Fun Item 1
	Game 2
	Fun Item 2
	Bible Text
	Announcements
	Interview
	Worship Time
Section 2	Bible Lesson
Preaching	Illustration 1
Time	Illustration 2
	Illustration 3
	Story
	Prayer

- After one minute the eight join with another eight and pray that God will...
- And so it continues until you have one very large group. You then pray for the whole group

The Hand

The Church of England website suggests using the following:

Your **fingers** can be used to bring your mind different things to pray for.

- **Thumb**
  This is the strongest digit on your hand. Give thanks for all the strong things in your life, like home and family, relationships that support and sustain you.

- **Index finger**
  This is the pointing finger. Pray for all those people and things in your life that guide and help you – friends, teachers, doctors, nurses, emergency services and so on.

- **Middle finger**
  This is the tallest finger. Pray for all the important people who have power in the world, like world leaders and their governments, members of parliament and local councillors, and the Royal Family.

- **Ring finger**
  This is the weakest finger on your hand. It cannot do much by itself. Remember the poor, the weak, the helpless, the hungry, the sick, the ill and the bereaved.

- **Little finger**
  This is the smallest and the last finger on your hand. Pray for yourself.

⇨ **Praise (7 minutes)**

Some lively songs. There are two slots for praise. Make sure you use the first slot for songs they know which contain lots of actions. New songs can be introduced in the second section. Some of the children may not enjoy singing – make it worth six points for best team singing, and suddenly you'll find they enjoy it a lot more.

	Programme
Section 1	Welcome
	Rules
	Prayer
	Introductory Praise
	Game 1
	Praise
	Fun Item 1
	Game 2
	Fun Item 2
	Bible Text
	Announcements
	Interview
	Worship Time
Section 2	Bible Lesson
Preaching	Illustration 1
Time	Illustration 2
	Illustration 3
	Story
	Prayer

⇨ **Game 1 (5 minutes)**
Games differ from week to week. But the following points are important:

> ## TIP
>
> **During the first section until preaching time music is present almost all the time – quiet, ambient music for explaining rules, loud music for games. The contrast of total silence in preaching time seems to help the children listen and focus on the discussion.**

- In order to play a game they must answer a question on last week's lesson
- Choose one person from each team and then allow that person to choose the rest of the team
- Give points for the teams that cheer people the loudest
- Play music while the game runs: fast music; live music if possible. If not, CDs
- The first team to complete the game must sit down

⇨ **Praise (10 minutes)**
The second praise slot allows for a longer session with several songs being used together. Encourage banners, streamers, dancing, etc. Allow some of the children to form a praise group that stands with a microphone to lead the others. I have included a list of good songs and music for children in the Recommended Resources Appendix.

⇨ **Fun Item 1 (5 minutes)**
We use several fun items to enhance the programme. Be creative with your ideas.

Guess The Leader
We use this slot to play a game called "Guess The Leader". We reveal an interesting fact about one of the leaders, or one of the children. For example, "This leader used to live in Spain". Then four leaders are chosen who all try to convince the children that they used to live in Spain. The children then have to "Guess The Leader" who really was telling the truth. A variation on this theme is to show a picture of the leader as a baby and the leaders all have to try to convince the children that they are the person in the picture.

		Programme
	Section 1	Welcome
		Rules
		Prayer
		Introductory Praise
		Game 1
		Praise
		Fun Item 1
		Game 2
		Fun Item 2
		Bible Text
		Announcements
		Interview
		Worship Time
	Section 2	Bible Lesson
	Preaching	Illustration 1
	Time	Illustration 2
		Illustration 3
		Story
		Prayer

Strip Search

Here is an idea from Saturday-morning television that helps with getting to know the children or leaders. Play some background music and then for one minute ask the leader questions about their preferences:

- Awake or asleep?
- Music or reading? The child/leader will then choose one each time.
- Chocolate or fruit?
- Kylie or Robbie?

Here are some sample questions to be used:

- Sweets or chocolate?
- Shoes or trainers?
- Bath or shower?
- McDonald's or Burger King?
- Cap or hat?
- Dogs or cats?
- Spring or autumn?
- Pepsi or Coke?
- Cinema or video?
- Morning or evening?

Buy It or Bin It

A chance for music and video reviews. It gives the children a chance to bring in the videos they watch and the music they listen to. It may not seem overtly Christian, but it is incredibly educational! Form a panel of three which includes one leader and two children and allow them to

		Programme
	Section 1	Welcome
		Rules
		Prayer
		Introductory Praise
		Game 1
		Praise
		Fun Item 1
		Game 2
		Fun Item 2
		Bible Text
		Announcements
		Interview
		Worship Time
	Section 2	Bible Lesson
	Preaching	Illustration 1
	Time	Illustration 2
		Illustration 3
		Story
		Prayer

view three videos/CDs for 30 seconds each. Then ask them if they would buy them or bin them, and why. Periodically introduce Christian music. It teaches the children critical thought, which is very important for their development. Don't allow the children to get away with "because it's good" or "because I like it" – they must at least try to explain why. They need their attention drawn to the lyrics: ask if they know what the song is about.

Who Wants To Be A Chocoholic?
Based on the television game show *Who Wants to Be A Millionaire?* A child is chosen from the audience. They are asked questions with increasing degrees of difficulty. They are given four answers to the questions and have to choose the right one. For a correct answer they gain more chocolate; for a wrong answer they lose it all. The trick is to know when to quit and take the chocolate. The children have lifelines – they can ask the audience or ask a leader. There are only two lifelines.

Aerobics Workout
A piece of music is played and the children copy the leader at the front performing their aerobic workout.

Double Dare
A child is chosen. The child then chooses a leader. The child will then choose between seven different envelopes. In each envelope there is a question; some easy, some very hard. The child will then make a decision before the envelope is opened: will they answer the question or will the leader? The envelope is opened and the question is asked of whoever the child chose. If the child chose to answer the question but gets it wrong then she gets a shaving-foam pie in the face. If she gets it right then she gets to place the pie in the leader's face. If the leader answers the question, the same rules apply in reverse.

This slot can also be used for all sorts of fun items such as puppet skits, etc. Use it to have fun with the children.

	Programme
Section 1	Welcome
	Rules
	Prayer
	Introductory Praise
	Game 1
	Praise
	Fun Item 1
	Game 2
	Fun Item 2
	Bible Text
	Announcements
	Interview
	Worship Time
Section 2	Bible Lesson
Preaching	Illustration 1
Time	Illustration 2
	Illustration 3
	Story
	Prayer

⇨ **Game 2 (5 minutes)**

Make sure that different people are involved in game 2 from the ones involved in game 1.

⇨ **Fun Item 2 (5 minutes)**

⇨ **Bible Text (3 minutes)**

We display the memory verse on the OHP from the start of preaching time and refer to it frequently, but you may prefer to encourage the children to memorise the text. There are many ways to teach a Bible text, and a few ideas are highlighted, but there are literally hundreds. Be creative.

- Write the Bible text on balloons and burst the balloon as the verse is read
- Make the verse into a jigsaw puzzle
- Write the verse on an object which communicates its message, ie, "You are a light to my path" can be written on a lamp or on a drawing of a bulb

	Programme
Section 1	Welcome
	Rules
	Prayer
	Introductory Praise
	Game 1
	Praise
	Fun Item 1
	Game 2
	Fun Item 2
	Bible Text
	Announcements
	Interview
	Worship Time
Section 2	Bible Lesson
Preaching	Illustration 1
Time	Illustration 2
	Illustration 3
	Story
	Prayer

- "The Lord is my shepherd" can be written on five cut-out sheep
- Laminate the verse onto lots of tiny sheets of paper and give each child one to take home

Remember that memorising the verse is not as important as understanding it. They may win a prize by being able to quote "The Lord is my shepherd", but it will change their lives if they understand it.

⇨ Announcements (2 minutes)
Summer camps, play schemes, colouring competitions, birthdays, special events, etc, all need mentioning here. If you are going to do birthdays then you must be consistent – don't do birthdays one week and then miss them out for two weeks; some children will miss out and feel hurt.

⇨ Interview (5 minutes)
Invite one of the leaders or one of the children to come and tell the group what Jesus has done for them, how he's helped them in work/school, how he cares for them, how they first made their decision to become a Christian. If the person is very nervous, interview them. If they are more confident, allow them to speak freely – taking notice of the timing allowed for this section.

⇨ Preaching Time
The rest of the programme falls under the heading "preaching time". This will include all worship, Bible lessons, illustrations and story. Take three minutes to explain the rules.

Time for a very special announcement. Inform the children that they are now moving into preaching time, which is the most important thing that happens. Inform them that this section can change their lives. There are special rules:

When the whistle blows next, preaching time has begun. In preaching time:

- Nobody leaves to go to the toilet. In fact nobody moves
- Anyone talking loses six points straight away without discussion

However, a leader will be walking around with tuck-shop tokens or sweets and will place them in the hands of anyone who really deserves one:

		Programme
	Section 1	Welcome
		Rules
		Prayer
		Introductory Praise
		Game 1
		Praise
		Fun Item 1
		Game 2
		Fun Item 2
		Bible Text
		Announcements
		Interview
		Worship Time
	Section 2	Bible Lesson
	Preaching	Illustration 1
	Time	Illustration 2
		Illustration 3
		Story
		Prayer

- You must be excellent to receive one. Good is not enough; anyone can be good
- You must keep facing the front. If you look at the leader (who we refer to as a quiet seat-watcher) they will not give you a token/sweet
- If you get a sweet/token and play with it (or try to open it) then it will be taken off you

Sweets and tokens are given sparingly. Maybe a sweet/token every three to four minutes. More than this changes the giving of sweets/tokens from an incentive to listen into a distraction.

⇨ **Worship (10 minutes)**
A quieter time of worship songs can be introduced. Encourage the children who know the words to close their eyes and begin to think about King Jesus. Take your time here, it is important to introduce them to worship.

Instruct the children that praise is generally loud and lively, a time where we have fun singing to God. Worship is where we come closer to God, and think about God more. Worship comes from our hearts and our minds. It involves all our emotions. The definitions of praise and worship may be much broader and more theological than this, but a bite-size theological portion is more easily swallowed by an eight-year-old.

Blow the whistle at the end of worship and inform the children again that this is preaching time (the whistle can be put away now; it will no longer be needed).

⇨ **Bible Lesson (5 minutes)**
There are various ideas to help with the presentation of the Bible lesson

- Dress some of the children up as characters in the story
- Use videos. The Recommended Resources appendix will give you some ideas
- If you are presenting the story in narrative form then tell the story as Hollywood would; don't just read the account

⇨ **Illustrations 1–3 (5 minutes each)**
Illustrations can take many forms.

		Programme
	Section 1	Welcome
		Rules
		Prayer
		Introductory Praise
		Game 1
		Praise
		Fun Item 1
		Game 2
		Fun Item 2
		Bible Text
		Announcements
		Interview
		Worship Time
	Section 2	**Bible Lesson**
	Preaching	**Illustration 1**
	Time	Illustration 2
		Illustration 3
		Story
		Prayer

● Object Lessons

An object can be used to communicate a truth. For example:

Objects Needed   A light bulb and a sheet of paper

People are always complaining that we are wasting things. Turn off the light, you are wasting electricity; use the back of that piece of paper, don't waste paper. Don't leave the tap running, you are wasting water…

All these things are important, and we mustn't waste things. But I heard a story once of someone who wasted something even more important. It was an old lady and she said one of the saddest things I have ever heard. She said that God had told her when she was young that she should be a missionary for him and go to a faraway country. The old lady said that she hadn't gone because she had found something else to do, and now she felt that she had wasted her life.

It's bad to waste money or electricity or paper or water. But it is the saddest thing in the world to waste a life. Being a Christian may be tough sometimes, but at least we will not waste our lives.

● Short Drama Sketches

Short drama sketches are an excellent way of communicating themes. Here's an example:

Cheese: Hi, everyone. It's me, the amazing Cheese. Has anyone seen the Chalk dude, he's not been around for a while? He's doing his exams.

Chalk: Hi, old chap! Did I hear you talking about me?

Cheese: Yes, I was just wondering when you're going to be back around playing and things. I've missed you over the last couple of months. All that work you've been doing for those exams.

Chalk: Yes, it's been quite difficult. I've had to work really hard. I've got to pass three different exams and then I get this really cool certificate that says that I am really clever.

	Programme
Section 1	Welcome
	Rules
	Prayer
	Introductory Praise
	Game 1
	Praise
	Fun Item 1
	Game 2
	Fun Item 2
	Bible Text
	Announcements
	Interview
	Worship Time
Section 2	Bible Lesson
Preaching	Illustration 1
Time	**Illustration 2**
	Illustration 3
	Story
	Prayer

Cheese: So you've done two and you've got the last one really soon?

Chalk: No! I've had enough now. I've been working really hard and those two exams were really long and I don't want to do any more.

Cheese: But dude, if you don't do the last exam then you won't get the certificate.

Chalk: That's true.

Cheese: Well go and do the final exam.

Chalk: I don't want to, it's too much effort.

Cheese: But you've done two already, you're nearly there.

Chalk: No, old bean, I'm not going.

Cheese: But, Chalk, this is foolish!

Chalk: Yes it is, but it's not as foolish as promising to do something for Jesus and then giving up halfway through.

Cheese: Well, I know it's not *that* foolish, but it certainly is foolish.

Chalk: Well, I guess you're right. I'll do the final test. I guess I'll see you soon.

Cheese: Go for it! We can always play next week.

What about you? Are you a good finisher or did you just start well? How many of you will finish the work God has given you to do?

● Video Clips

With a video camera, go to the streets and get a teenager to interview passers-by. Passers-by can be asked if they believe in God, if they own a Bible, what they understand by the word "trust".

● Commercial Movie Clips

Video clips can also be used to communicate. Here's a clip from the movie *Hook*.

This is one of my all-time favourite movies. It's the story of when Peter Pan grows up and goes back to Neverland and finally defeats Captain Hook and saves his children. There's a great bit towards the end.

Hook has been defeated and Peter stands opposite Tinker Bell and Tinker Bell says to him:

"So Peter, I guess your adventures are over now."

Peter looks at Tink and says these words:

	Programme
Section 1	Welcome
	Rules
	Prayer
	Introductory Praise
	Game 1
	Praise
	Fun Item 1
	Game 2
	Fun Item 2
	Bible Text
	Announcements
	Interview
	Worship Time
Section 2	Bible Lesson
Preaching	Illustration 1
Time	Illustration 2
	Illustration 3
	Story
	Prayer

"Tink, to live is an adventure."

And those people who will give their lives to Jesus and allow God to do whatever he wants with them will discover that living for Jesus really is an adventure.

● Testimonies: Personal Testimony

Things that happen to us often illustrate important truths, and here's an example:

I had to go on a journey once to a place in the north of the country. I got on a train very early in the morning and was on my way. We hadn't travelled very far when it started to snow. It kept on snowing and didn't look as if it was ever going to stop snowing. When I was halfway there I had to change trains. When I got off my train the whole world had gone white. The snow kept on falling and most of the trains were cancelled. There were just a few trains left running; one was going back towards my home and another was going in the direction I was heading but not exactly the right way.

I had to make a decision. It would have been the easiest thing in the world to get back on the other train and go home. But I didn't. I got on the other train. You see, I had friends waiting for me, and I didn't want to let them down. I got on the other train.

God is desperate for us to finish the journey we started with him. He doesn't want us to turn back; he wants us to keep going.

The train took me to somewhere near where I wanted to go and then I had to get in a taxi and travel the last 40 miles. The taxi couldn't get me all the way. So in the freezing cold and well after midnight I had to walk the last bit. And then to my horror I discovered the person I was going to stay with wasn't there. He hadn't been able to get home because of the snow. I had to phone someone else and only eventually found someone to stay with. But I had got there. I didn't turn back. I finished the journey. I reached the destination.

God didn't tell us it would be easy serving him: in fact he promised that it would be hard at times. But we must keep going.

	Programme
Section 1	Welcome
	Rules
	Prayer
	Introductory Praise
	Game 1
	Praise
	Fun Item 1
	Game 2
	Fun Item 2
	Bible Text
	Announcements
	Interview
	Worship Time
Section 2	Bible Lesson
Preaching	Illustration 1
Time	Illustration 2
	Illustration 3
	Story
	Prayer

When we start something, we need to see it through until the end.

● Testimonies: Stories of Others

Not only are stories about our own lives useful, but things that happen to others can also be an excellent communication tool:

Once during the American War of Independence an accident happened as several of the American troops were travelling along a muddy path. A wagon they were using had overturned and was blocking the road. The captain of the troops had lined up several of the men and was shouting at them to push and push and push to try to turn the wagon back over.

When the wagon wouldn't budge, the captain got even more annoyed and shouted louder at his men to push. After some time, a man on horseback arrived at the place where the wagon had turned over and asked:

"Captain, why don't you help these men rather than just shout at them?"

But the captain was amazed at the request.

"I am their captain," he replied. "I should not dirty my uniform in such a manner."

With that the man got off his horse. His uniform was already dirty. He walked over to the men and said:

"I will help! Let's push again."

Now, with the help of this stranger, the wagon was pushed upright.

The captain was glad that the wagon was restored but annoyed that this stranger should have interfered. As the stranger got back onto his horse the captain demanded:

"Who are you, sir? What gives you the right to interfere in my affairs?"

The man on horseback smiled. "I am General George Washington, and I interfere because you are in my army. And from now on, Captain, you will lead by example."

The captain didn't know how to answer. So he simply said:

"Yes sir!"

That day the captain learned the importance of leading by example. Do we give a good example for others to follow or not?

	Programme
Section 1	Welcome
	Rules
	Prayer
	Introductory Praise
	Game 1
	Praise
	Fun Item 1
	Game 2
	Fun Item 2
	Bible Text
	Announcements
	Interview
	Worship Time
Section 2	Bible Lesson
Preaching	Illustration 1
Time	Illustration 2
	Illustration 3
	Story
	Prayer

Basically, anything that will help to present the overall lesson can be placed here.

⇨ Story (15 minutes)
A modern parable which rolls all the themes presented so far into one neat narrative package. Again, there are various methods that can be used to enhance the presentation:

- Use some of the children as characters in the story
- Draw some of the characters to use as flash cards or acetates
- Keep it dramatic, use your body and voice to maximise the presentation
- Some of the stories that you plan to use can often be given to an artist to illustrate. From there it is fairly simple to photocopy onto acetate for display on your overhead projector. For the more computer-literate (and those who own a video projector) you can scan the pictures into your computer and use a package such as Microsoft PowerPoint™ to display them
- Use crowd actions or a mimed response to certain words

⇨ Prayer/Response (5 minutes)
Always ask for a response. Make an appeal. Ask the children who felt the lesson applied to them to stand. If it required forgiveness, pray a prayer of forgiveness together. Let the children respond by repeating the prayer after you. There should be a response.

COMMENT

Don't underestimate the importance of standing at the door and saying goodbye to the children and parents. Parents need to see a person they can relate to and once again the emphasis is on the establishment of long-term relationships. Say goodbye, allow them to ask questions, allow them to clarify with you when the Christmas/Easter special begins. Allow them the opportunity to ask about how their child can get involved in a small group – all this by simply standing at the door.

⇨ Next Week (3 minutes)
Highlight next week's programme. Keep it exciting: "Next week everyone who comes will get a cream egg", "Next week we'll hear the concluding part of this exciting story", etc.

⇨ **The Finishing Touch (2 minutes)**

Ask a leader to dismiss the children a row at a time. Head for the door and say goodbye to the children; talk to some parents. Mix!

Programme Enhancements

It's always the little things that help make the programme just a little more special. Ideas such as keeping a diary of the club's activities and appointing a diary committee. Taking the children on outings. This takes a lot of organisation, but can be a lot of fun and can help form some excellent relationships. Use your creativity. These things are the icing on the cake.

The Extra Stuff

- Programme Formats
- Sample Schools Letter
- Sample Lesson Plan
- Five-Year Planner
- Leading a Child to Christ
- Sample Leaflet
- Colouring Competition
- Sample Lesson from *IMPACT*
- Legal Issues and Child Protection
- Recommended Resources

These programme formats are included to give an indication of the magazine style of presentation that is being used with this generation of children.

FORMAT FOR "LIVE & KICKING" (BBC 2000)

1. Introduction
2. On Today's Show
3. Live Music
4. Interview
5. Cartoon
6. Karaoke With Leprechauns
7. Phone-in Game
8. Music Video
9. Competition
10. Cartoon
11. Competition Winners
12. TV Sitcom Preview
13. Feature: Hobbies
14. Quiz: Guess the Person
15. Interview
16. Skit From Leprechauns
17. We've Got Your Number
18. Sitcom
19. Coming Soon
20. Sitcom
21. Coming Soon
22. Talent Slot
23. Your Letters
24. Cartoon
25. Interview
26. Movies, Games, Reviews
27. Interview, Feature
28. Skit From Leprechauns
29. Word Up Challenge: Billy Connolly
30. Music Reviews
31. Game
32. Phone-in Questions
33. Winners of Talent Slot
34. Next Week
35. End

- **Programme Length: 165 minutes.**

"SESAME STREET"
(Children's Television Workshop)

1. Elmo going to meet Prince Charming
2. Titles
3. Elmo meets Prince but he's on the cellular phone
4. Elmo meets Prince but he's on the fax
5. Elmo meets Prince but he's on the normal phone
6. Elmo meets Prince but he's on the answerphone
7. Prince Charming is stressed and resigns
8. Video – telephone ringing in street
9. Animation – talking, walking telephone
10. Video – two children make a map of neighbourhood and then explain their map
11. Animation – the letter K: kangaroo, kite, etc
12. Video – the city garden project
13. Puppets – dance and rap
14. Humans chatting about poems
15. Interview – Big Bird meets a poet: what is a poem, a game with words
16. Animation – toothpaste
17. Video – how to clean your teeth
18. Animation – I love my teeth
19. Song – toothbrush song

- **The programme has only been on for 15 minutes.**

FORMAT FOR
"THE SATURDAY SHOW" (BBC 2002)

1. On Today's Show
2. Live Music
3. Cartoons (Part 1)
4. Game – Gutbusters
5. Cartoon (Part 2)
6. Game – Potshot (phone-in game)
7. Interview
8. Quiz – Know Your Knose
9. Cartoon (Part 1)
10. Game – Postshots
11. Puppet Skit
12. Sketch – Sausage Family (1)
13. Interview
14. Docu-soap – Stamford Amp
15. Letters
16. Cartoon (Part 2)
17. Game – Risk
18. On Today's Show
19. Game – Risk (2)
20. Sitcom – Big Wolf on Campus (1)
21. Quiz – Who Are Ya!
22. On Today's Show
23. Quiz – Lady Loo Loo Challenge
24. Live Music
25. Game – Pants Win Prizes
26. Sketch – Sausage Family (2)
27. Quiz – Fan Face Off (1)
28. Cartoon
29. Sitcom – Big Wolf on Campus (2)
30. Interview
31. Sketch – Sausage Family (3)
32. Quiz – Fan Face Off (2)
33. Game – Thumbs on Phone
34. Music Video
35. Puppets read e-mails
36. Game – Thumbs on Phone results
37. Video Review – Winner Stays On
38. Cartoon
39. Quiz – Fan Face Off (Final)
40. Video Review – Winner Stays On
41. On Next Week's Show
42. Live Music

- **3-hour programme**

Cartoons and sitcom take up much time. The other items are two to three minutes long.

FORMAT FOR SMTV LIVE (ITV 2002)

1. Fun Beauty Contest with SMTV presenters
2. On Today's Show
3. "Ring To Win" Quiz
4. Live Music
5. Eat My Goal – celebrity guests try and score goals against SMTV presenter for viewers
6. Interview – with famous person
7. Quiz
8. On Today's Show
9. Moan! Moan! Moan! – Viewers' Letters
10. *Sabrina Part 1* (children's television programme)
11. Who Lives in a Brain Like This (Through the Keyhole gone crazy!)
12. Live Music
13. On Today's Show
14. Brian's Brains
15. Eat My Goal
16. *Sabrina Part 2* (children's television programme)
17. FOGBOUND Drama skit by presenters
18. SMTV Wannabe – child wins a place at a West End show
19. Music Video
20. On Next Week's Show

90-minute running time: *Sabrina* accounts for 30 minutes; commercials take up a lot of time. The rest of the items are between two and four minutes long.

SAMPLE SCHOOLS LETTER

ST MARY'S, BLETCHLEY
Church Office, Church Green Road,
Bletchley, Milton Keynes
01908 000000
mark-griffiths@st-marys-bletchley.com

Thursday 24 April 2003

Dear Head teacher / Assembly Co-ordinator

Re. Assemblies For Primary Schools

The last academic year was interesting to say the least. We have taken nearly 100 assemblies a term, taken several harvest presentations to parents, several carol concerts for parents and old folk, and a number of those ever-interesting OFSTED assemblies – we now have over 20 OFSTED assemblies completed. So, here is the first assembly series of the new academic year:

JANUARY – BECAUSE HE TRIED

People thought it was impossible to run a four-minute mile until Roger Bannister did it, then many others ran in under four minutes. People thought Everest couldn't be climbed until Edmund Hillary climbed it – then many others climbed it. Sometimes when we think something is impossible we never actually try. The mountain's too big, the distance too great... Sometimes when we try we discover that things open up in front of us, just because we tried. This is the story of George and his determination to become a lawyer even though he and his family have never left the farm.

FEBRUARY – GREEN NOSES

A return to Max Lucado's Punchinello stories – you may remember the first story "You are Special". If not this isn't a problem, the stories are independent. The Wemmicks have all started painting their noses green so that they can be like the other Wemmicks. Individuality is the main theme of this assembly.

MARCH – THREE TREES

This assembly has been used in many places by many different people, but it is still very popular. One day a farmer plants three very special seeds. Three trees grow tall and strong. Every day they discuss what they want to be when they are eventually chopped down. They all have big ambitions. But the fulfilment of those ambitions is beyond their wildest dreams. The Easter story is woven into this assembly.

Booking assemblies for the next three months is a simple process of picking up the phone between 9am and 12 noon any day and working out three suitable dates with our administrator. If you are part of a combined school I can come in twice or we can do back-to-back assemblies. The choice is yours. There is no charge for this service as it is very much a part of our vision to be a positive part of our community. I will also endeavour over the next couple of months to visit each of the schools within the parish to see if we can be of further service as a church.

Your truly
Mark Griffiths

SAMPLE LESSON PLAN

FORMAT:

	Programme	**Item**
Section 1	Welcome	
	Rules	
	Prayer	
	Introductory Praise	
	Game 1	
	Praise	
	Fun Item 1	
	Game 2	
	Fun Item 2	
	Bible Text	
	Announcements	
	Interview	
Section 2 **Preaching Time**	Worship Time	
	Bible Lesson	
	Illustration 1	
	Illustration 2	
	Illustration 3	
	Story	
	Prayer	

OVERVIEW:

FIVE-YEAR PLANNER

	Year 1	Year 2	Year 3	Year 4	Year 5
September					
October					
November					
December					
	CHRISTMAS				
January					
February					
March					
	EASTER				
June					
July					

● Develop one assembly each month, to be repeated in all the schools you visit that month. At the end of the month write up the assembly. After five years you will have enough assemblies to continue to repeat assemblies on a five-year rotation.

LEADING A CHILD TO CHRIST

GOD	YOU
God is **LOVE** – 1 John 4:16 God is **FAIR** – 2 Thessalonians 1:6 God is absolutely **PURE** – 1 Peter 1:16	We were created good, but became **SINFUL** – Romans 3:23 We deserve to be **PUNISHED** for doing wrong things – Romans 6:23 There is **NOTHING WE CAN DO** to fix it – Isaiah 64:6
JESUS	**RESPONSE**
JESUS is **GOD**, who also became man – John 1:14 Christ died as our **SUBSTITUTE** – 1 Peter 2:24 Christ offers his forgiveness as a **FREE GIFT** – Ephesians 2:8–9	You and I must **RESPOND** – Romans 10:13 We must ask Christ to be our **FORGIVER AND LEADER** – 1 John 1:9

SAMPLE LEAFLET

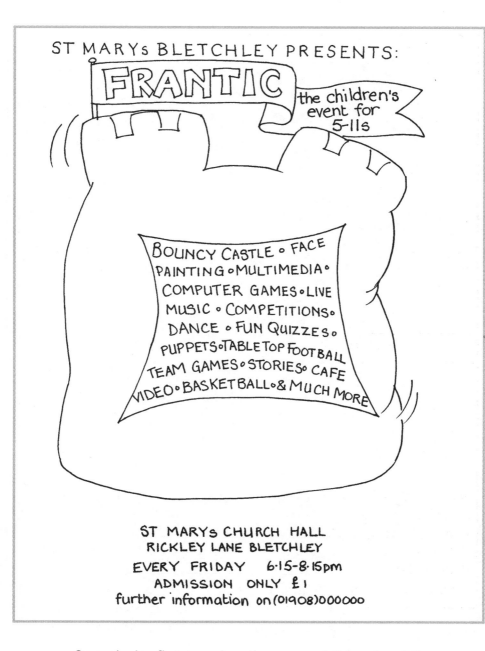

ST MARYs BLETCHLEY PRESENTS:

FRANTIC

the children's event for 5-11s

BOUNCY CASTLE ○ FACE PAINTING ○ MULTIMEDIA ○ COMPUTER GAMES ○ LIVE MUSIC ○ COMPETITIONS ○ DANCE ○ FUN QUIZZES ○ PUPPETS ○ TABLE TOP FOOTBALL TEAM GAMES ○ STORIES ○ CAFE VIDEO ○ BASKETBALL ○ & MUCH MORE

ST MARYs CHURCH HALL
RICKLEY LANE BLETCHLEY
EVERY FRIDAY 6·15-8·15pm
ADMISSION ONLY £1
further information on (01908)000000

Sample leaflet to advertise your children's club

My Kids' Club
COLOURING COMPETITION
To be returned on Friday evening at the start of children's club

Name: _____

The best colouring will win a prize

Sample handout for home visits

Beginnings

	Programme	Item
Section 1	Welcome	
	Rules	
	Prayer	
	Praise	
	Game 1	Lego 1 – Order Out Of Chaos
	Praise (x2)	
	Fun Item 1	
	Game 2	Lego 2 – Towers
	Fun Item 2	
	Bible Text	Genesis 1:2
	Announcements	
	Interview	
	Worship (x2)	
Section 2	Bible Lesson	Genesis 1
Preaching	Illustration 1	*Toy Story 2*
Time	Illustration 2	Formless And Empty
	Story	Carlos (1)
	Prayer	

Overview It started with God bringing order out of chaos, creating a world of perfection. But God has a flare for the dramatic, and Genesis 1:2 is the build-up before the explosion. The world was empty and dark, with the Spirit of God hovering. Something was bound to happen – God was there. And the same God hovers over the lives of children, waiting to explode.

Game 1

Lego 1 – Order Out Of Chaos

PREPARATION   A pile of lego for each team, placed at B.

PLAYERS   Four players per team.

SET-UP   Players stand at A.

OBJECT   The players run from A to B, create "something" out of the chaotic pieces of lego within two minutes and then bring their creation back to A.

WINNING   The team with the best construction wins.

Game 2

Lego 2 – Towers

PREPARATION   As for Game 1.

PLAYERS   Four players per team.

SET-UP   The lego pieces are placed at B.

OBJECT   The first person races from A to B, collects a piece of lego (only one piece) and returns. This continues until all the pieces are collected. While the pieces are being collected someone at A attempts to construct the tallest free-standing construction with the pieces.

WINNING   The tallest free-standing construction wins. Remember: free-standing – the towers must not be held.

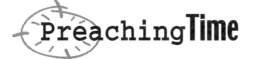

PreachingTime

BIBLE LESSON   **GENESIS 1:1 – 2:4**

"The earth was formless and empty, darkness was over the surface of the deep, and the spirit of God was hovering over the waters." (Genesis 1:2, New International Version)

Genesis is the very first book in the Bible, and it's where we will be spending most of our time for the next couple of weeks. It has some great accounts of Noah and his ark, of Abraham and Isaac, and of Joseph and his coat of many colours. All these are found in Genesis. But right at the start of Genesis is a very special account indeed. It is the story of creation – of how it all began. It tells of how God created day and night and animals and plants and flowers. Listen as I read you the first verses from the first book in the Bible:

In the beginning God created the heavens and the earth. The earth was barren, with no form of life; it was under a roaring ocean covered with darkness. But the Spirit of God was moving over the water. God said, "I command light to shine!" And light started shining. God looked at the light and saw that it was good. He separated light from darkness and named the light "Day" and the darkness "Night". Evening came and then morning – that was the first day.

God said, "I command a dome to separate the water above it from the water below it." And that's what happened. God made the dome and named it "Sky". Evening came and then morning – that was the second day.

God said, "I command the water under the sky to come together in one place, so there will be dry ground." And that's what happened. God named the dry ground "Land", and he named the water "Ocean". God looked at what he had done and saw that it was good. God said, "I command the earth to produce all kinds of plants, including fruit trees and grain." And that's what happened. The earth produced all kinds of vegetation. God looked at what he had done, and it was good. Evening came and then morning – that was the third day.

God said, "I command lights to appear in the sky and to separate day from night and to show the time for seasons, special days, and years. I command them to shine on the earth." And that's what happened. God made two powerful lights, the brighter one to rule the day and the other to rule the night. He also made the stars. Then God put these lights in the sky to shine on the earth, to rule day and night, and to separate light from darkness. God looked at what he had done, and it was good. Evening came and then morning – that was the fourth day.

God said, "I command the ocean to be full of living creatures, and I command birds to fly above the earth." So God made the giant sea monsters and all the living creatures that swim in the ocean. He also made every kind of bird. God looked at what he had done, and it was good. Then he gave the living creatures his blessing – he told the ocean creatures to live everywhere in the ocean and the birds to live everywhere on earth. Evening came and then morning – that was the fifth day.

God said, "I command the earth to give life to all kinds of tame animals, wild animals, and reptiles." And that's what happened. God made every one of them. Then he looked at what he had done, and it was good.

God said, "Now we will make humans, and they will be like us. We will let them rule the fish, the birds, and all other living creatures."

So God created humans to be like himself; he made men and women. God gave them his blessing and said: "Have a lot of children! Fill the earth with people and bring it under your control. Rule over the fish in the ocean, the birds in the sky, and every animal on the earth. I have provided all kinds of fruit and grain for you to eat. And I have given the green plants as food for everything else that breathes. These will be food for animals, both wild and tame, and for birds." God looked at what he had done. All of it was very good! Evening came and then morning – that was the sixth day.

So the heavens and the earth and everything else were created.

By the seventh day God had finished his work, and so he rested. God blessed the seventh day and made it special because on that day he rested from his work. That's how God created the heavens and the earth.

Toy Story 2

Object needed: *A video clip.*

Play the introductory scenes from Toy Story 2 – *you'll know which part to play and where to stop from the narrative that works with it below.*

That was a small clip from *Toy Story 2*. It is before all the action really gets going and before Woody's adventure really begins. It shows just a quiet, ordinary bedroom. Some of you may live quiet, ordinary lives; maybe the action hasn't got going yet. But for those who will let God be part of their lives, the adventure is yet to begin.

Formless And Empty

Objects needed: *Modelling clay, Flash paper*, matches.*

The whole story of creation is wonderful, but I particularly like the first part: "The earth was formless and empty, darkness was over the surface of the deep, and the spirit of God was hovering."

"The world waformless and empty." Let's use our imaginations. Imagine "formless and empty". That would be like this modelling clay: no

shape, no form, of no real use. How about, "darkness was over the surface of the deep"? *(Turn the lights off and ask for complete silence.)*

Then the spirit of God was hovering. *(Light a match.)*

You see, when the spirit of God is hovering, you can be pretty sure that something is going to happen. And the spirit of God is hovering over your lives tonight, lives that may seem to have no shape or form, lives which are dark because of that stuff called sin – the junk, garbage, rubbish in our lives. But God's hovering. He's about to do something. He wants to do something.

And the spirit of God hovered over the formless and empty earth and then God said, "Let there be light". *(Light the flash paper.)* And there was light. *(Put the lights back on.)*

God wants to take your life, which you may feel is empty and a bit formless, and make it into something remarkable.

So in a way, we are like modelling clay. It is formless, it has no real shape, like many of our lives. But it is God who puts the shape and form into us. He gives us purpose – we use a big word: destiny. This means becoming what God wants us to become.

* Flash paper is available from Paul Morley Supplies on 01706 649921.

● STORY – Carlos (1)

Carlos sat down in his bedroom and looked around the sea of beds in the dormitory. There were fifteen beds in all. It was crowded, but comfortable. All the boys who shared the dormitory had their own cupboard for storing their things – not that Carlos had many things. He had two pairs of trousers that had been given to him, two T-shirts, a jumper and a sprinkling of underwear and socks. Oh, and the coat that one of the older boys had kindly given him because it didn't fit him any longer.

Carlos looked into the mirror fastened

to his cupboard. He stared. Two bright blue eyes stared back. He began to dress for bed. He put on his boxer shorts and looked at himself in the mirror one more time. He was hoping that his muscles would arrive soon, but there didn't seem to be any signs yet. He flexed his right arm, but there really was nothing there – nothing, that is, except Carlos' strange mark. On the top of his left arm there was a very curious shape. It looked like a wave splashing into the air. Carlos often wondered what it was, but recently had decided it was just a birthmark. Carlos crawled into bed and lay back on his pillow; he pushed his long, curly blonde hair out of his eyes  and stared up at the ceiling. Carlos was nine years old. The place he lived in was not his real home, but it felt like home to him. He grabbed his stuffed rabbit, which by now was looking a bit worse for wear, snuggled it under his chin and began to drop off to sleep.

Carlos' earliest memories were very happy ones. He remembered being rocked to sleep by his father, and the feel of the cot blankets on his face. His fondest memories were of looking up into his mother's radiant blue eyes as she sang to him a song about cows jumping over moons, and plates running away with spoons.

The little stuffed rabbit was his only reminder of that time now. Somehow that world had vanished away from him, and now he lived with many other boys and girls in an orphanage run by monks. Carlos lay on his bed thinking, little realizing that everything was about to change.

LEGAL ISSUES AND CHILD PROTECTION

Legislation affecting children's clubs and the very serious issues associated with child protection are outside the remit of this book. The rules change with infuriating frequency and the procedure to ensure your club/project has the proper policies in place can be a minefield. The best I can do is point you in the direction of the experts.

For all you need to know about writing a clear child-protection policy, contact:

Churches' Child Protection Advisory Service
PO Box 133
Swanley
Kent
BR8 7UQ

Tel: (0845) 120 45 50

Also, it is certainly worthwhile owning a copy of:
"A Policy on Child Protection – A policy document of the House of Bishops" published by SPCK.
This is worth having whatever your denominational affiliation.

For help on other legal issues, including police checks, contact:

Criminal Records Bureau
Disclosure Services
PO Box 110
Liverpool
L3 6ZZ

Tel: (0870) 90 90 844

For help with Data Protection issues contact:

Information Services
Data Protection Registrar
Wycliffe House
Water Lane
Wilmslow
SK9 5AF

Tel: (01625) 545 745

RECOMMENDED RESOURCES

MUSIC

Children of the Cross	Jim Bailey	Kingsway
God's Gang	Jim Bailey	Kingsway
King of Heaven	Doug Horley	Kingsway
Shout to the Lord Kids 1 & 2	North Point Church	Integrity
Whoopah Wahey!	Doug Horley	Kingsway
Lovely Jubbly	Doug Horley	Kingsway
Any of Ishmael's Collections	Ishmael	Kingsway
Soul Survivor Collections	Compilation	Survivor Records
Extreme Worship	Jim Bailey	Kingsway

SCHOOLS

52 Ideas for Junior Classroom Assemblies	Chris Chesterton and Pat Gutteridge	Monarch
52 Ideas for Infant Assemblies	Chris Chesterton and Elaine Buckley	Monarch
Lion Storyteller Bible		Lion Publishing

BOOKS

77 Talks for 21st Century Kids	Chris Chesterton	Monarch
77 Talks for Cyberspace Kids	Chris Chesterton and David T. Ward	Monarch
Fusion	Mark Griffiths	Monarch
Impact	Mark Griffiths	Monarch
Reclaiming a Generation	Ishmael	Kingsway
Devil Take the Youngest	Winkie Pratney	Bethany House
Fire on the Horizon	Winkie Pratney	Word
Streets of Pain	Bill Wilson	Word
A Theology of Children's Ministry	Lawrence O. Richards	Zondervan
The Prayer of Jabez for Kids	Bruce Wilkinson	Tommy Nelson Inc
Come Holy Spirit	David Pytches	Hodder & Stoughton

HOLIDAY CLUB MATERIAL

Kim's Quest	Mark Griffiths	Monarch

VIDEOS

The "VeggieTales" Series	Big Idea Productions	Word
The "Testament" Series	Bible Society	Bible Society
The Miracle Maker	Bible Society	Bible Society

NURTURE RESOURCE

The "Y" Course for Children		Scripture Union
God Stuff	Doug Horley	Energise Publications

RECOMMENDED WEBSITES FOR RESOURCE MATERIAL

www.kingdomcreative.co.uk
www.ishmael.org.uk
www.jubilee-kids.co.uk
www.armslength.com

www.duggiedugdug.co.uk
www.kidzblitz.com
www.tricksfortruth.com
www.treasureKids.com

PUPPETS AND GENERAL

For a spectacular range of puppets visit **www.armslength.com** or from
www.tricksfortruth.com

SUMMER CAMP

For information on interdenominational Summer Camps for children check out
www.treasureKids.com, **www.new-wine.org** or **www.scriptureunion.org.uk**

SHORT-TERM MISSION

King's Kids offer short-term mission opportunities for children and can be
contacted via the Youth With A Mission website **www.ywam.org**

CONTACT

If you would like Mark Griffiths to come and talk to your children's leaders or
you have any observations on this book, please contact me on
mark-griffiths@st-marys-bletchley.com or **markgriff@lineone.net**